MOMMY REBELLION

BRUTAL HONESTY ABOUT MOTHERHOOD AND OTHER SH*T WE PRETEND WE LOVE EVERYTHING ABOUT

CHASE YOUNG

TESTIMONIALS

"This is a book to let moms know they aren't alone in the magical mess, to help them know it's okay to be a mess, make a mess, and choose how you're going to get through the adventure of motherhood." – R. M. Vallance, author and mom of 4

Find her at https://amzn.to/2EoW9rz

"I would describe this as an easy, enjoyable, touching, relatable read. I recommend this book because it's really funny while at the same time being really true. You know *all* those Mom moments you don't really talk about and wonder if you are the only one that deals with them? Well Chase bares the glorious AND messy sides of parenting in this book and you will feel *so* seen, that you are not alone, and be able to laugh at how absurd and hard parenting is sometimes." – Lisa Presley, Productivity Pixie and mom of 1

"This is a book that tells it like it is and helps you to know that whatever you're going through you're not alone. Parenting is messy and that's okay." – Jennifer Moore, Modern Medicine Lady, author, faery godmother to many

Find her at www.modernmedicinelady.com

"Everything you're thinking but too afraid to say for fear of judgment. But we've all been there." – Katie Gall mom of 1

Find her at www.keepingitrealkatie.com

Dedication

To my mother for showing me the way.

To my daughters for teaching me how to be a mother.

To Rob for being my partner on this messy parenting journey.

And to you, reader, for if you have ever felt alone, exhausted and grossed out by parenting, this book is for you.

CONTENTS

ACKNOWLEDGMENTS

Books are never written in a vacuum. And there are many people behind the scenes that help support the author in a myriad of ways.

I would like to thank Jen Moore for being my Fairy Godmother and helping this book from conception to publication and cheering me along the way.

Nikki Starcat Shields who is an amazing book midwife and who actually helped me figure out that I could write this book in 15 minutes 3 days a week and it took me less than a year to get all the words written down (editing is another thing that Nikki is amazing at!).

Britt Bolnick my business coach who helped me keep my eye on the ball and adjust timelines as needed, especially after my concussion in the winter of 2019. Thank you for all your kind love.

To Amanda Lopes–Bregoli for listening to me go on and on and helping me make sure my systems were good, my self–care masks were on and happily listening to me swear and being my roommate on various retreats.

Lisa Presley the Mommy Rebellion Ambassador for helping keep all the contributors to the blog in line and therefore freeing up my time to write this book, and for your constant support and laughter.

To my Beta readers who made this book better, Katie, Rachel, Jen, Lisa, Nikki, Britt, and Amelia. And to all the *9 Month Pathway* women, thank you for holding space for me and watching this process. You know who you are and I love you all.

To my girlfriends Cathy, Rachel, Allison and my mother who listen to me rant when I've had enough of my kids. And who will always help out when I ask for it from food to companionship to stealing my kids away for a while.

To my daughters who keep me laughing and have taught me just about everything I know about parenting.

To my hubby who kept cheerleading from the sidelines and who might someday actually read the book. Thanks for being my partner in all of this and understanding that when I start a sentence with "Your Child" or "Your Daughter" it's time for you to take over parenting for a while.

And to you readers, may you find some laughter and solace and give yourself the freedom to parent your way, in all the unique messy style that is yours!

INTRODUCTION

The Mommy Rebellion was born from a need for mothers to share what it truly is like to be a mother, and not just the pretty stuff we tell the world. Not just from the *oh my God my kid is grosser than your kid* perspective, either, but from the need to share even the mundane and boring aspects of being a parent.

Here it is 2019 and we live in a fast-paced digital world where time is how we measure our lives, down to the second (except perhaps when we are caught up in the social media rabbit hole). This book is a reflection of that and a reflection of Mommy Rebellion, and my business which I have built in 5 to 15 minute spaces of time. I have built it all and written this book in sections of time that took place in less than a half hour.

Because some days, even finding 5 minutes of peace is impossible.

I invite you to read this book as it was written, in small batches, one essay or poem at a time. I have grouped these essays around similar themes, like *Gross Things Our Kids Do*, *Seasons of Our Lives*, and *Rants*. Pick it up anywhere you would like and put it down when it has served its purpose.

As I am all about *putting your fucking oxygen mask on first*, I would recommend that you do some self-care around reading this book. Like maybe having a beverage that makes you feel good, perhaps in a locked bathroom or while taking a bath. Or heck, while your kids play outside; it's all good. Just remember that you have to refill your cup sometimes. Frankly, I have found that it is worth the guilt and feelings of unworthiness that crop up the first few times you serve yourself first to actually have a fuller cup to pour from. At the end of the day, your kids are watching your every move anyway, so why not have them catch you in the act of reading and taking care of yourself?

THIS IS MOTHERHOOD

REMEMBERING WHAT IT WAS LIKE

I remember what it was like. To be staring at the wall, nursing my baby again. Not being able to reach a book or a drink and needing to pee, but this small little girl is looking up at me or maybe dozing. I am the most important person in her world right now, and she is just nursing and sucking the life blood out of me. Or at least that's what it feels like at this moment. She is not letting me sleep, she is just nursing, and pooping and peeing and puking on me and I am not sure what day of the week it is or when I last took a shower – and did I mention I really need to pee?

She's not my only child. There are others that need attention and love and need to be kept alive. Kept alive. That is all I am trying to do right now – to keep everyone alive – but right at this moment I don't feel alive. No, not at all. I am so fucking bored that I have forgotten what boredom is, and that it exists, and that this is the state I am in. I am just so tired.

I started waiting pretty much from the moment I found out I was pregnant. It was like time started to stretch and a day became a week and a week a month and a month a whole year and everything just slowed down. I am not a happy pregnant person. No glow-y flowers for me. Nope, that's not me, and while my friends insist that I do glow when I am pregnant, as far as I am concerned it's like entering the longest form of hell imaginable.... I am taken over by this new alien creature.

So by the time I have endured 10 months of this and actually birthed this small miracle, I am already in such a state of waiting and absolute discomfort and well, boredom actually, that it's hard to know what to do anymore. I look forward to my hubby coming home from work, but once he is here, I am not sure what to do. He offers to look after the baby for a bit and while in some ways that is a relief, in others, she's only just finally gone to sleep and now he gets to cuddle and reap the benefits of her being asleep. Why is he so much better at getting burps out than I am?

Oh, and we have other daughters so as soon as he comes home and takes our smallest one, now they all want or need my attention and what about my needs? What are those like again? Oh, right I need to pee, there is that. Some food and something to drink might be nice. I dream of sewing or knitting or quilting again, of making something with my hands that does not involve food or laundry or spit-up.

Reading and not being interrupted, being comfortable - what does that look like? Moving without a toddler and baby strapped to me, or at least hanging off of me. I feel like I am drowning and I don't remember how to breathe and how did I get here again? No, seriously, how did I get here? How do I get out? I mean, if I admit that I am struggling, that I am failing, that I would like nothing more than to hide in the bathroom all day, they might take my kids away.

They might laugh at me. They might say, "you can't complain - you've given birth naturally and 'easily' outside of a hospital to a healthy baby girl so what are you complaining about? You have food and clothes and a roof over your head, so seriously, what are you complaining about? Everything should be perfect, you have a fucking husband for God's sake, who will cook and clean up baby spit and change diapers and hold babies, so really your life should be fucking perfect."

Only it doesn't feel that way. It doesn't feel that way from the inside. Admitting that, even to myself, feels like this huge weight of failure, like there is something wrong with me. Ignoring the fact that it is winter and I haven't seen the sun in days. Ignoring the fact that it is cold outside and that I look forward to running errands just to get out of the house but in the end it is so exhausting. I am so exhausted. Seriously, this sleep deprivation thing has got to be inhumane. I mean, like Guantanamo-Bay-level torture.

But we all go through it, right? Just like the bleeding for months after the baby is born that no one tells you about until after you are pregnant and in the last trimester, so there is no turning back now, baby, nope, not at all. Or at least no one told me, and I thought I came from a nice liberal background. You know, I knew about the birds and the bees before I was 4, I read *Our Bodies, Ourselves* as a teenager, and dammit, I'm liberated. I even thought about being a midwife as a career choice and yet here I didn't know I was going to bleed for four months after my baby was born. Four fucking months to make up for nine months of not bleeding. Doesn't seem fair to me.

Now wait a minute, where was I? Oh that's right. I am nursing this small creature. Who I love. Honest to

Goddess, I love her. I just wish sometimes that she needed someone else more than me. That I could sleep for more than two to three hours before she needs me again. And yes, I suppose if I had chosen to go the formula route maybe I would get more sleep, but why mess with a system that has worked for millennia? Giving me a little extra food to eat is way cheaper than buying formula and Jesus I am so sleep deprived I am sure I'd fuck up making a bottle anyway. This is just about getting my nipple in my baby's mouth. And yes, I know I am lucky that all my girls have been good at nursing pretty much instantly. Several have felt like chunks of glass coming out of my nipples when my milk came in, but by and large it has all gone smoothly and according to plan.

But seriously people, it sucks. This sucks. And I am so goddamn bored!!

THERE ARE DAYS WHEN BEING A PARENT JUST SUCKS

You know the days when you feel like all you do is clean up bodily fluids that really should stay in the body? That doubles if you have pets, because of course they decide to lose their bodily fluids all on the same day, because perfect storms are where it's at.

Lots and lots of puke, poop, pee, vomit and who knows what else – those are the days where everyone will agree with you that parenting sucks. No one will disagree with you, or say that you are crazy or that you should just love parenting. On those days, everyone just nods their heads and agrees that yes, on days like those, parenting does in fact suck.

But what about the other days when parenting sucks? When you feel like you have just earned the Worst Parent Ever award because you weren't paying 100 percent attention, or you had to be someplace other than where your kid needed you or you forgot that you needed to pick them up somewhere and they had to call you? What about those days? Are those the days you tell your parenting friends about while sipping your favorite beverage?

Or the days when you get out of bed and just drag your feet and really, if that child that you love, and look after and care for, says just one more word in that voice of theirs you just might lose it, whatever it was that you were supposed to have in the first place.

Or the days when you are just so bone tired because you were up all night, either because you were parenting or just because you were finishing that project, wrapping those presents, or prepping for the week ahead.

What about those days? Are those the times when you admit to your other mom friends that parenting sucks? That you have wondered at least twenty times that day why you ever thought being a mom was a good idea? Do you talk about those things at all?

Or do you just keep going? Pull up your big girl panties and just keep doing what you need to do and ignoring the fact that you feel like shit and that frankly life just isn't fun anymore?

I think this is when a lot of women start drinking, or binge-watching TV, or finding out how to take some Ritalin or something like that. I often try and figure out how I can hide out in the bathroom for at least an hour (probably in the bath reading a book) and just let them watch TV. Or go for a walk, or take them all out to the playground.

Some of us drink, some of us eat, and some of us have probably developed better ways of dealing with these feelings of disillusionment, discontentment, and just wanting to get past this shitty phase of parenting already.

But we don't often share how we are feeling because we are afraid of being judged. We're scared of being told that we are bad mothers, bad parents, that we aren't Pinterest Perfect. So we don't share. We don't tell our spouse how we are feeling, we don't tell our own parents and heaven forbid we don't tell another parent how we are feeling.

But what if we did? What if we came up with a badge or a secret handshake or a slogan that says, "You know what? Today parenting sucks." Today I could use a friendly smile, a hug, a knowing wave as an assurance that you too have days when you would rather be anything other than the parent of the child(ren) you are with. That it is okay to feel this way, it doesn't make you a bad parent, it just makes you a parent. Just like the best job in the world can have days that suck, this hardest job in the world can also have days that just suck. Or weeks. Or months. You can get through it and it doesn't make you a bad parent. You can get support and have people help you and admit that frankly, you can't do it all, and today you can't do most of it.

This is okay. Because we have all been there. We have all had moments when parenting sucked. Whether we admitted to it or not, it happened and we felt that way. I wonder how different the world would be if we started sharing these moments. If we let other mothers into the club. If we agreed that while there are wonderful days and moments with our kids (and let's hold on to moments, because with kids the perfect day does not exist with any more reality than unicorns), there are also the sucky ones. And it is okay to feel and admit to both.

It is more than okay. It is vitally important so we can support ourselves and each other. So that we can be whole.

POSTPARTUM DEPRESSION

I never expected to have postpartum depression. I am not sure if any mother does. But I certainly didn't – especially not after my third child.

It wasn't even immediately after having my third baby come out of me that I had the depression. The depression didn't start until she was six months old and then it hit me like a bullet train out of nowhere.

I had been working on elimination communication with my youngest. It had worked reasonably well with my first and second born and I had been working full time then so I thought it would work even better with my third child who I would be home with the whole time.

But bending down and leaning over the toilet to help her pee into it ended up doing a number on my knees, at the same time we were living in a two story house, something that was also different from the single story houses with my first two daughters....

It didn't work. I woke up one morning with excruciating pain in my knees and wondering how I was going to get myself and the baby down the stairs. To add to that, my eldest was not quite six, my middle was not quite four, so for all intents and purposes they were no help. Unlike previous times with small children, my husband was no longer working from home and was instead working outside of the home and on a night shift so he wasn't there to support me either.

We were fairly new into a move, and I had some friends, but not really people I had come to learn that I could in fact rely on.

What instantly went through my head was, "What if I can't carry this baby around? I can't get hurt and not be able to carry this baby because my husband has a back injury and isn't supposed to carry her around." At this point she was nearing 20 pounds, because I have big babies and she had been over 17 pounds at four months old, and his weight limit was 10 pounds. So I needed to be physically capable of looking after this sweet baby and my knees hurt.

I had to let go of the elimination communication and trying to teach her to pee on the toilet, because even sitting down on the stool while holding her was not helping my knees feel better. I already had to walk her for hours on my back at night to get her to go to sleep, praying that she would in fact stay asleep once I put her down or stopped moving.

In a word, I was exhausted, both physically and mentally. I didn't know what to do. I reached out to my midwife who had delivered her and she recommended fish oil and vitamin B supplements, which I started. That helped, but it didn't make the overwhelming weight of depression go away.

I was strong enough to let my husband know what was going on and to tell a couple of my new friends so they helped check in on me. We lived where we could walk into town, which required walking back up the hill to get home, which is not the easiest thing when carrying a baby on your back, pushing one child in a stroller and listening to the other child complain, but it can be done. We only had one car at that point, and with three kids that needed car seats, it was not always the easiest to just go to the beach or the park to get a change of scenery.

It took several months for me to move past this deep depression. What actually got me out of it was something I would have never guessed. It was 2012 and the great Massive Online OC courses had come into being. Coursera had started up with all sorts of free classes you could take online. I signed up for a Science Fiction and Fantasy literature course and a couple of other ones, just to have something adult to do and to think about – and guess what, apparently that was exactly what I needed. I was bored, so very bored that I didn't even realize it, but as soon as I had that adult-level content to be doing, to be reading, to be learning about, the great fog of depression started to lift.

I needed some adult time, thinking about adult things (though I hate to use the word adult, because there was no sexual content in any of this). What I needed was something unrelated to my children, unrelated to my husband, and unrelated to taking care of children. Hanging out with other imperfect moms was super helpful too, but having something that was mine, that engaged the thinking part of my brain, that was what in retrospect really saved me. It led me to wanting to run my own business so I could earn my own money so that I could be contributing to the family economy on my own terms and in my own way. There were the things that were important to me. This is what helped me come out of my depression.

While I kept a close eye on myself after the birth of my fourth child, depression didn't come knocking at my door again because I had things in place to keep my brain busy and to keep me from feeling like just a milk machine.

INTERRUPTING CHICKENS

There is a picture book called *Interrupting Chicken* that was first shared with my family during a story time at one of our local libraries. The librarian, who enjoyed singing songs and reading books to the kids, apparently hated to use puppets, but for this book she got out a small finger puppet of a chicken because....

As the little chicken is getting ready to go to sleep she asks her Dad to read her a story. He starts one of the classic fairy tales, and before he has gotten too far into the story the little chicken interrupts and retells the story with a happier ending. This happens the magical three times before the Daddy chicken gives up and tells the little chicken to tell the next story – whereupon the Daddy chicken promptly falls asleep.

It's a very enjoyable picture book, whether you tell it with a chicken puppet or not, and my family has borrowed it from the library several times.

But the power of these stories, whether they are things that happen in real life, or that we tell ourselves, or that we pick up from beloved books, TV shows, and movies, is when they become shortcuts to explaining our lives.

Interrupting chickens has become code in my family to mean that the kids have not let me or my hubby finish anything we have started that day. It explains how frustrating it has been to try and help them get their needs met while simultaneously getting what we need to get done, done.

There are other shortcuts in my family. *1201* is code for when you are so overwhelmed by emotion or sensory input or noise or whatever that your brain just wants to (or actually does) shut down and you need a few minutes of quiet to reboot yourself. This comes from a trip to Kennedy Space Center and learning that 1201 was the code that the computer in the lunar lander sent to NASA right before Neil Armstrong had to take over piloting the lunar lander so they could land safely on the moon. The computer got overloaded with information and had to reboot 50 feet from the ground.

Another one is *I am undecided about spots*, which is hard to explain if you've never watched the British version of the sitcom *Coupling*. Toward the end of the last season, the couple has an argument over whether their new couch cushions should have spots or stripes. But in my marriage it has come to mean that we really don't care and could the other person just make the decision, please. It is helpful to have shorthand for this, especially in public where someone might think we should both have an opinion about something.

Troll droppings is a nice way of saying all the shit that ends up everywhere in the house the moment your child becomes mobile. It also includes the stuff the cat drops on the floor or the dog leaves lying around. *Troll droppings* is the morass of stuff that is on the floor and really needs to find its way back to its home or get dumped in the trash. Seriously, where do they find all this stuff to leave on the floor? It can also include sticky fingerprints and mud tracked through the house. Pretty much anything an adult didn't leave behind. Think *Family Circus* with *Not Me* and *I Don't Know*, their friendly household poltergeists.

Do you have code in your family? Are there shortcuts that explain things? Do you nerd out and answer the kids, when you are going for a family drive and they want to know where, that you are *taking the second star on the right and going straight on until morning*? Do you occasionally draw out the word legendary with a *wait for it* in the middle?

What is the family lexicon in your life?

SUICIDE WATCH

One of my favorite quotes about parenting is Michael J. Fox saying that parenting is like a constant suicide watch. You are just trying to keep your kids safe and prevent them from doing something that will kill them.

I think this is especially true at certain ages. Toddlers, definitely. Until around four, for my kids, when it starts to get a little bit better. Of course, it depends on the child, too. My youngest has been on suicide watch since she became mobile at about 5 months old. She is probably the reason we have not had any more kids up to this point. Every time I think about it, she goes and does something that is so *her*, but reminds me that I don't think I could handle another one doing even close to the same shit.

I think that there are probably suicide watches in the teenage years as well. I don't officially have a teenager yet, so I can't swear to it, but I suspect there will be some. I know that the forgetfulness that seems to come with the hormones could be a suicide watch in and of itself if they were having to look after things that really mattered and it wasn't simply a matter of getting chores done in any kind of timely fashion.

Since the concept of teenagers is so new, as is the science of how long that brain is not fully developed (well into the twenties and in some cases thirty), it makes you wonder how the species even survived when until recently teenagers got married, moved out, and started having kids. Maybe that's why in some cultures women moved into their husband's parents' house. Maybe that was to make sure the next generation did survive. So that the older women made sure the new babies got looked after even if the teenage moms were less than ideal.

I am not sure. I just know that there are periods of time where my hubby and I look at each other after a long day of intense parenting, and go, "they are all still alive!" Not everything may have gone quite according to plan, but at least they are all still here and breathing. Most of the time they are pretty healthy, too. We've had our share of emergency room visits, but the most major illness they have had is the chicken pox. That was just a long summer of being quarantined, more than anything else. It was really only 72 hours each of misery for the girls. Just wait until they meet heartbreak.

So yes, toddlers. Every time I think about how lovely a newborn can be (and let's face it, the cute little things are usually depriving everyone in the house of sleep), I remember what toddlers are like. I used to think that just getting my children to age 3 and then again to age 5 was huge, and "yay me, they are still alive!" But I have to admit that as my girls get older and need more of my mental space, I think maybe just keeping toddlers safe might have been slightly easier. At least their needs were easier to determine. Now they seem so much more complicated, and sometimes I don't think my brain is up for it.

Suicide watch. I am not even going to go into all the chemicals and drugs we are now giving our children so their behavior is easier to deal with. I am not going there with a ten foot pole because 1) I don't have personal experience with it, and 2) every situation is going to be different. I just think medication that plays with moods is going to bite us in the butt one of these days. But perhaps I read too much science fiction and spend too much time outside.

Speaking of which, we need to stop unpacking and start going hiking again. It's summer and I have missed it! After this weekend, when we host our first open house party (which is mainly so we have a deadline for getting most of the house set up and organized), I think we should go back to hiking every weekend. There are some new hiking trails we could explore, and some new fun to have. For my older girls, taking them on a hike does seem to be an important part of suicide watch. As in, all that hiking outdoors seems to prevent suicide. Maybe that is what we are missing as a society. Not enough time outdoors. Because let's face it, taking toddlers outside does usually keep them happy for hours and while they do get filthy, they are usually reasonably safe.

Being outdoors seems to calm my older kids down as well. Maybe we should find a hammock. Then we could all spend more time outside. Resetting our earth clock.

WE TIPTOE SILENTLY ACROSS THE FLOOR

We tiptoe silently across the floor
Ever watchful of the sounds we make
Ever hopeful that they will stay asleep
Just a few moments more
Or hours so we can rest.
While their head rests steady on their pillow
We peek in to check on their breathing
And slowly slink away.
We will cause damage to anything
That makes too loud a noise
And wakes our slumbering child
Prematurely
Or at all.
We will call out the huge
Mama Bear
That lives inside
To anyone who decides
To throw a party, make a bang,

That fireworks should remain
Going off after our child
Has gone to sleep.
We will drive for miles to keep them
Sleeping in their car seat
Even past the point where we too need to sleep.
We will stand and hold them,
Rocking,
Rocking,
Afraid to stop moving because they will wake.
Even when they are older
And sleeping when we need them up,
So we yell up the stairs
Or outside their doors
Reminding them that it is in fact time to get up,
There is a part of us
That needs the quiet,
That wishes we could let them sleep,
That feels relief knowing that our
Watch is on pause.
That we are keeping them safe
And alive
But that we don't actually have to engage
With or worry about
Them
Because they are asleep.
And when they sleep we can relax
On a deeper level than we could
When they were awake.
And maybe, just maybe,
If we time it right,
We can also get some sleep in
While they are sleeping
Or some reading
Or just sitting and breathing
In the fact that

They are asleep
And we are now finally
Mostly
Off duty.

Default Parent – Parenting is Boring

When I first became a parent I was the breadwinner. It wasn't necessarily planned that way, but my hubby injured his back at work when I was about three months pregnant and the ensuing workman's comp mess meant that by the time our first daughter was born, I was the only able-bodied parent that was still working.

At that time I was working in a fabric store part time. Before my firstborn was a year old, I was working full time and my daughter was staying either with my Mom or with my hubby, depending on how his back was feeling and what shift I was working.

I was super lucky. My bosses were fine with my daughter coming in at my lunch break of half an hour and my nursing her in the break room. I pumped on my 15-minute breaks. The only time I had to "myself" was the ten-minute drive to and from work. That was it.

I loved being able to connect with my daughter during my work day, though it got harder and harder for her as she got older and missed me more. We kept this routine up until I quit, right before we moved away to Maine, so this was the experience that both my two daughters had in their first few years of life.

For a while it was perfect – after my second daughter was born, I worked the 6 am to 2 pm shift and came home just in time for nap time. It worked out well for all of us, as I would fall asleep at nap time with my girls. That lasted for not quite a whole year and moving back to a constantly-changing shift schedule was hard on me, my body, my girls, and my relationship with my hubby.

Shift work is pretty horrible, but is standard fare in retail these days if you work anywhere that is open past 6 pm. My store was open until 9 pm, so I could close one night only to have to open the next day. There was no guarantee that I would have two days off in a row. Working retail really does suck.

But it was all my first two daughters knew. It was their reality that Mummy would go to work most days, they would come in to see her at her meal break and nurse and cuddle, and then possibly see her when she got home.

Their Dad and Grandma and Uncle and Grandfather were around more. Their Uncle and Grandfather also worked, though usually more consistent hours. I am sure they must have created routines, but I do not know what they were, because I wasn't there.

I do know that my eldest whined and fussed more when I came home. Apparently there is this phenomena of the safe person that you show all your unhappy feelings toward, and that was me. I was her safe person, so I was the one (and to a certain extent still am) that she moans and groans to. It was frustrating to me, though, that the only time I got to spend with my daughter she was whining at me. It was super frustrating.

All I dreamed about, almost every day, was getting to be a stay-at-home mom. I longed to be the parent who stayed at home with my kids. My hubby is a great father, but he needed time to work on his business so that he wasn't doing it late at night when we were all trying to sleep and then he needed to watch the girls the next morning because I had work. That is not sustainable in the long term.

That is what we worked for. Part of our goal of moving to Maine was that I got to stay home with our two daughters. I got to be the stay-at-home parent while my husband continued to build his online business. That was the plan and the big dream.

But you know how they say *be careful what you wish for*? I don't regret moving to Maine. We love it, even though we have had some hard moments. Those happen in life, no matter where you live.

What I wasn't expecting was how boring being the stay-at-home parent to small children is. My girls were four and two when we moved to Maine, and in less than a year I was pregnant with our third child. By the time we were entering our fourth year in Maine, we had four daughters, and while I had built an amazing community of friends, I was amazingly bored.

It took me a while to admit these things to myself. Just like it took me a while to let my ego get out of the way enough to realize that my eldest daughter needed a Girl Scout leader that wasn't me, because she had me all the time since we homeschool. That getting that exposure to other adults leading is actually something I seek out for my girls as the opportunities present themselves.

I was shocked and ashamed when I first realized how bored I was. No one really talks about it. No one wants to admit that looking after small people in isolation is very boring, with unpredictable periods of intense stress. You look forward to the other partner coming home or finishing up work, but they are tired too, and may not react the way you want them to.

I am still amazed when I read in books about spouses trading off who is in charge of the kids. I am not sure what that would be like. I think by and large my hubby and I have worked out a pretty good system. We each try to get time away alone, as well as to co-parent when we are together, and clearly communicate when we need the other person to be in charge of the meals, the decisions, etc. We work together to not be too busy with social events, but to not stay at home all the time either, striking the balance for our family with what works right now.

WE MUST FEED THEM

Children must be fed. It's part of the job description of being a parent. You must feed and water your kids and make sure they sleep and take them to the doctor and dentist every now and then, and make sure they wear shoes, at least in the colder months. These things are all part of not being neglectful of your children.

But where is the fucking guidebook? Where is the recipe plan to feed your children? No wonder the food industry has been able to get so many fucking chemicals, high fructose corn syrup, and other things down our kids' throats. Anyone who has ever tried reasoning with a small person over food knows exactly what I am talking about.

I miss nursing. Not actually having someone attached to my nipple, I am so done with that, but the ease of having the perfect food for my child at the perfect temperature, right there ready for them when they were. It was bliss for them and it was so much easier than arguing with a preteen who needs to eat.

I want my kids to eat good food. We are building a homestead so we can grow better food for them than we can afford to buy in the quantity a family of six needs. This is why we have ducks that lay eggs, bacon seeds growing in the brambles, and meat birds ready to be harvested in about six weeks. I do this for them! If I didn't have them, I could probably afford to just buy locally organic food as it is and not have to grow it all myself. Yes, we would grow some of it, because my hubby actually enjoys gardening. As for me, I feel like it's just one more thing I need to keep alive, most of the time....

But it's not that simple. For instance, my kids are on a breakfast strike again. It doesn't matter what I offer them, someone isn't going to want to eat it. You know that I feel that breakfast should be a *serve yourself and leave me alone and let me drink my coffee and read a book* kind of meal, right? The perfect weekend morning with hubby is when we communally make some yummy food and then eat it on the back porch while drinking our coffee and not necessarily exchanging a word.

That's what breakfast should be, not a drama or a tirade. I am not awake enough to deal with temper tantrums. Please just find something that doesn't have a lot of sugar in it and eat it! Part of this is coming from breakfasts while we had company staying with us, where I actually bought a shit ton of cheap (and therefore nasty) bread and made toast every morning that they slathered in peanut butter. Or we had granola with yogurt, which is not something I usually stock because my kids could go through a quart of yogurt in a snack, let alone a meal! My budget doesn't stretch to that. It just doesn't. Not when most yogurt is devoid of any food–like substance and will give my kids a massive sugar high.

So this morning I thought I would nip the whole issue in the bud. I thought I would go ahead and cut up some of those first Maine apples that we were given from friends yesterday, and add in some duck eggs, and oatmeal, and pumpkin spice seasoning (because I couldn't find the straight cinnamon) and mix it all up and it would be yummy.

It sure smelled yummy to me. But my kids rejected any bit that looked like it had touched an egg. Maybe I didn't mix it well enough, or maybe there was not enough water to the oatmeal, but I expected those juicy apples to leach out their juices. Maybe I should have cooked it on the stove instead of in the microwave, but I wanted to get my coffee and breakfast made as well.

I don't the fuck know.

All I know is that two out of four kids rejected it out of hand and the other two just pickily ate around the eggs. Thank goodness the pigs will eat it. But that's it. I said I was done helping with breakfast at that point. They could have peanut butter on a spoon, another apple, make themselves a new batch of oatmeal, but please leave me the fuck alone.

Okay, I left the fuck part out of the sentence, because I try not to traumatize my kids too early in the morning. And well, I guess the smell of coffee had started having an effect.

But oh my Goddess, they had better come up with a good idea for breakfast tomorrow, because I am so done with this. I am so tired of this. I think maybe I should make them breakfast the night before, when I am fucking tired from getting dinner on the table.

That's what the Pinterest moms do, right? Or they get up super early to make a yummy breakfast for their kids? That's what you find on Instagram, right? Not me. When I get up before my kids I am going for a walk with my audiobook, or sneaking up here to get some writing done. I am not making glorious breakfasts unless it is someone's birthday, or a holiday, or we are having brunch guests and games. Just not fucking going to happen.

I guess this is how all the boxed cereal companies stay in business.

Pass the fucking milk.

EARLY MORNING SNUGGLES

One of the best aspects of parenting is snuggling. That cozy time where your body touching their bodies is simply enough. When they don't necessarily need to talk (though of course sometimes they do) but simply need to be held.

As I write this, my 11-year-old who, has been coming to sleep at the end of my bed for weeks now due to who the heck knows what, but she's not waking me up in the middle of the night, so eventually she will move past this, has just woken up. None of her sisters are awake yet and it's before 8 am, so she's decided to climb into bed next to me and snuggle.

I explained that I needed to write, so she isn't speaking. She may be reading over my shoulder, I am not sure, but there is a sense of coziness to her just hanging out next to me.

I am sure this would fall under the Danish concept of *hygge*, of doing things to just feel really cozy and connected. I suppose if we had a candle burning or were near a fireplace and it was wicked weather outside that would make it even better. Instead it is the start of another sunny spring day.

But right now it is still quiet. The only sounds are our breathing and my light tapping of the keyboard on my laptop as I write this. There are some distant traffic noises, as we live not far from one of the major routes here in Maine.

Her eyes have drifted closed so I know that right now at this moment all is good in her world. Her needs are being met. Let's face it, as parents, that is something that should be celebrated and appreciated, that right now things are good.

No emergencies, no fighting, no hysterics. Right now, things are good.

When my babies were, well, babies, one of the best parts of my day was when they would fall asleep on me. I would be content just holding them for hours (oftentimes in a baby carrier, especially after my firstborn), knowing that all was good in their world, that I had done everything they needed me to do.

When they were toddlers and so into exploring their worlds, and at times it felt like a never-ending high-alert suicide watch, I would hold out for when they would take a nap. Even if sometimes it was on me and they were all sweaty and hot and I was all sweaty and hot. It created such a good connection, such a good bonding experience to have them sleeping on me and knowing that once again everything was good. I could take a deep breath and just relax for a while.

When my daughters were little, and where we lived was small, my hubby would often reconnect with them when they slept on him. It was the favorite part of his day, too. His love language is touch and I am not sure there is much in the world that makes him happier than having a slumbering small child on his chest. I really think that is one of his favorite parts of being a father.

But children grow. We want them to, because that means they won't stay in this stage that is driving us crazy forever. As they grow, it can be so easy to lose that connection, to lose that time to be in touch with the other person. I don't have sons, so I don't know if it is different than with daughters, but there comes a point where you really have to wait for them to ask for hugs, rather than them giving them as often and with such free abandon as they did when they were little. Hugs become almost sacred.

I used to do something we called the "lap thing" when I got too big to fit in my mother's lap. There were just two of us, my brother being 3 ½ years younger than me, and my mom would read us many a chapter book aloud as part of our homeschooling (though I am pretty sure she would have done it even if we had remained in school longer). Anyway, it was often an after-lunch cozy time and we would put our heads on either side of her lap while she was reading. Often giggles and silliness would ensue.

But what I remember most, other than getting the opportunity to stare at the ceiling for hours on a regular basis (which really does change your perspective of the world) was that we had that regular physical connection. We had that regular touch.

My girls often jostle over who gets to sit next to me on our too-small couch when we watch television together. Some days, honestly, I am touched out and need to go sit someplace else. I do my best to help everyone have a turn and make sure that the ones whose turn it isn't know that most likely at least one of them can curl up by their Dad. There seems to be something so important about these snuggle times. Just like curling up next to my hubby at night is often the highlight of my day.

She has fallen so far asleep that she is snoring, which she needed. I am sure my bed has got to feel better to her body than the floor. It feels really good to have this connection time with her. One that doesn't require my brain to be on. One where my mere presence is simply enough.

I am enough.

For her.

Right now.

I am going to sit here and breathe that in for a while.

THE VISIBLE PARENT

Visibility.

It is something I think we all struggle with. Because we are women, because we are mothers, because we live in a society that cares so much about what we look like. We are immediately judged and are judging everyone on how we look.

It is written in our DNA. We are supposed to find the people who look like us so that we can be protected as babies. So we can be cared for and nurtured. So that we can belong and therefore be loved.

Yet if you have any small part of you that is an introvert, if you have ever told a secret in confidence and had that confidence spread like wildfire, then you have met up with issues around visibility.

It is not always safe to be visible, and as women we inherently know this, even if we fight against it. We have been oppressed in so many different ways for so long, that we know this. We know this.

It isn't always safe to be visible as moms. I remember having my young daughters point out the truth of things. My butt was getting big because I was pregnant and they told me about it repeatedly.

They watch my every move, all the time, from the moment they wake up until the moment they go to sleep, and they have been doing this since the moment they were born. They will always be doing this. This was the burden I picked up when my first daughter was born. This constant watching, and being the model for everything. Because that is what our role is as mothers, there is no real getting around it. We can deny it and pretend it doesn't exist, but it is still there.

Lately, I have been noticing more gray hair. It could just be that I inherited the early gray hair gene that runs in my maternal line. Or maybe life has been stressful lately and this is the way my body is choosing to express it. As a redhead, it is not as obvious as it would be if my hair was darker.

So far my daughters haven't commented on it. But I wonder, if my gray keeps coming, if my youngest will remember me with red hair. What gifts of visibility will I be handing off to her?

I constantly work with visibility in my business, in writing a weekly blog post and posting a weekly video on Facebook. So far I am not going to lie and say it has gotten any easier. What comes up each time changes, but easier? Nope.

Being visible in the current world is not always easy or safe.

But the more we can be, the more we can shine our light in the darkness, it may help more women, daughters, mothers to shine their light as well.

How does visibility affect *your* parenting?

THESE GIRLS OF MINE

These girls of mine
I never dreamed
that you would all appear
so fresh and new
and wrinkly too
with folds of fat
and fuzzy heads
one after the other
I took care of you
I still take care of you
but my have you grown
what was once one
became two
three
four
And here you all are
in your loud
exuberance
and voices
singing in choruses
You are so full of life
and fights at times
too numerous to count and
yet
I know
That you love each other
with the deep-rooted passion
That only siblings can have
That sisters can have
You against the world
Strong girls.
Silly girls.

I can't imagine life
without them,
my darlings,
my dears,
these girls of mine.

FAMILY VALUES, AND I DON'T MEAN SEX

You should totally have family values about sex,
too.... Or at least discussions about it as a family. I
don't believe that avoiding the conversation with your
partner or your children ever leads to anything good.
But that isn't what I want to talk about here.

Here I want to talk about what other values your
family has. Have you thought about them? Have you
gotten your family involved in the discussion?

It can be as simple as buying one of those family
rules posters/photo frame things. You know, the one
with phrases like *Love More*, *Hug Often*, *Clean Up After
Yourself*, *Say You're Sorry*, that kind of thing. That can be
a great starting point for the discussion.

But what does your family believe in? What is
important to you as a family? It can start with the
things you love.

You have probably guessed from reading this book
that my family loves hiking, camping, and adventures.
We also love playing games, reading aloud as a family,
and watching movies. We find family time together (all
six of us) important, which is why we try and have
every Sunday as a stay-home day for all of us.

Family time is important to us.

So is honesty. Which as parents means that we have to control our emotions when our kids tell us that they broke something, because kids start lying because they want their parents to be happy. We have tried (and the jury is still out as to whether we have failed at this or not) to say that we would rather know the truth so we can help you fix it, than stay happy not knowing what is going on. I totally had the Universe call me on this last week, when I was pretty sure my 10-year-old had broken the key to the new freezer and my 5-year-old had stepped on a window pane and broken it on the same day. Hubby handled that one a lot better than I did.

What about unplugged time? Does your family put down their electronics regularly, or even just at the dinner table? Looking after animals and growing our own meat has become part of our values as a family. I hope to get the vegetable-growing underway next year.

Is doing the right thing even when it's the hardest thing important to your family? Do you talk about trust, and courage, and how you feel about politics? Is going to your house of worship important to you?

What is important to your spouse or your kids? Have you sat down and asked them? I bet you might just be surprised by what they have to say.

I'd love to be part of this conversation, so let me know what you think. Contact details are at the end of the book. Come on over and join the discussion!

JUST ANOTHER DAY: MOTHER'S DAY 2017

Mother's Day.

The universe doesn't remember that today is supposed to be a special day, unlike any other.

Little babies or even toddlers can't suddenly change who they are. Right. Now.

So on this Mother's Day,

I still woke up in a puddle of pee, something that hasn't happened in *months*.

The rain was pouring from the sky so badly

That me and the five-year-old got soaked just walking to the van.

I still had a headache and felt off due to allergies and travel.

BUT

I had a great time shopping with just one of my children. The grocery store gave her a red carnation to give to me....

Not that she wanted to, because well, they did give it to HER, after all.

My hubby got me a pop-up card with flowers on it because that way they wouldn't make me sneeze.

My 10- and 8-year-olds made me cards all by themselves, spelling and penmanship errors included.

Dinner was yummy, and just as noisy as always.

The kids still didn't want to go to bed at bedtime.

I was still exhausted by the end of the night and fell asleep before hubby came to bed.

It's those little things

That don't just happen on Mother's Day.

But can happen any day

If you just look for them, and hear them.

It's the 3-year-old saying *I Love You* as she leaves the room.

It's the 10-year-old's attempt to wash all the dishes even if she missed the ones on the table in the other room.

It's the way the 5-year-old smiles, just for me.

It's the way the 8-year-old tries and tries and tries again to perfect that next set of monkey bars.

I won't remember this Mother's Day next year.

I won't need to,

Because as mothers, every day has the gross and urgh, as well as the beautiful.

You just have to know where to look.

And after 10 years of being a mother

I'm okay with that.

It's a whole lot less pressure this way.

And way more realistic.

Gross Things Our Kids Do (Like Eat)

Breakfast

Breakfast should not be a meal. Or at least not a meal that I need to be social at. Surely breakfast is a leisurely meal with a nice hot drink, some yummy food, and a book to read, or barring that, some nice adult company. I don't mean adult as in *50 Shades of Grey* adult, I mean adult as in, you know, an actual conversation that you can have without big explosions, or spilling of milk and then crying over the spilled milk (yes, that does actually happen, kids do cry over spilled milk, especially if it hits their clothes or that happens to be the last of the milk in the house). But an actual adult conversation.

I dream of old couples eating their toast and reading their newspaper in silence. That seems to be almost the perfect way to eat breakfast.

Not. My. Reality. Nope. Doesn't happen here.

Here I often eat before the kids do, if I manage to drag my ass out of bed before they get up. Which in theory I like to do, and I do – I like having a few moments of peace before everyone else gets up, I really do. Unfortunately the moment one of my kids gets sick, or I get sick, or one of the kids decides to interrupt us in the middle of the night with nightmares, or heaven forbid move into bed with us, that seems to fly out the window. I mean, I would love to drag myself out of bed at 5:30 or even 6 am, but between that and making up for all the sleep I just lost, I am afraid the sleep almost always wins out. And yes, I go to bed before 10 pm almost every night, because I don't know about you, but these kids are making me old, or I am just old or something. But in any event, I am in bed by 10, usually around 9:30, and lights are off by 10:30 at the absolute latest, thank you very much.

I have even worked hard to create a sleep sanctuary in my room, you know, with blackout curtains, plants to help clean the air, and no blue screens for me after about 9 pm. My hubby might be scrolling on his phone in bed, but I am not. I am back to real actual books, thank you local library. I exercise. I do all these things in the hopes of not waking up at 3 am and being unable to go back to sleep, because that seems to be my lot in life since probably when I first started having kids. Now I worry that it's early, early onset menopause or that it will only get worse when they become teenagers. Maybe I should just get used to it. But I don't jump on my tablet, I don't turn on the light, I do use the bathroom and then I move on to trying to go back to sleep.

So yes, getting up first thing in the morning happens sometimes, more often in the summer than in the dead of winter when I need more sleep just to get through the day (I am going to just stick to the biological research on this and say stuff it people, I am sleeping). But I still try not to eat breakfast with my kids, because 1) we don't eat the same things and 2) I love them, truly, but kids are gross eaters even at ages

4,6,9 and 11 and frankly can put you off your food anyway.

My 11-year-old whines that she doesn't want to eat alone without a grown up. Because younger sisters apparently just don't cut it. So I do sit with them, usually with the four-year-old on my lap eating her breakfast, and while that can be gross I usually don't have to see more than the back of her head.

Our latest compromise (because what is life if not compromise?) is that I read them a book while they are eating breakfast. When I can get away from being a lap I will often chair squat, or stretch my legs out and wander around while I am reading aloud to them. I am usually pretty antsy to start my work day, but read aloud to them I do. And it helps. It allows us to read more than just Harry Potter, which we started about 6 months ago and are still only in book four (because that's a 700-odd pager and will be the longest read-aloud I have done with my children, if we ever finish it, so help me God!). Knowing them, even the death of a character in this book is not going to stop them from wanting to read number five. Thankfully we own the whole collection so at least I don't have to worry about library due dates; that's a whole other discussion for another time. Seriously. More librarians need to be parents of small children to remember what it is like to try and keep track of all those flipping books!

I still daydream of quiet adult breakfasts. Like when my Dad and I were in France and we got to just sit and eat chocolate chip croissants and drink black tea (because to my American palette, French coffee was nasty) and have a leisurely breakfast. I still dream about that. Only with my hubby, and no kids, and it doesn't even have to be in France. The backyard in the sun would do, and we do find it sometimes. I mean, the kids are usually around, we've just already fed them and sent them out of the room. I am usually overly hungry from waiting for a chance to actually eat with a grown up. But hey, at least we get that in most weekends, on at least one morning.

That's what I think about while trying to make it through another breakfast as a solo parent. I hold on to the weekend morning breakfasts, or the ones in my head when my hubby and I will run away for a long weekend. Those are coming eventually, right? Right?

MUD AND PEANUT BUTTER

My kids are muddy monsters. I don't know how many times I have to remind them to leave their muddy things, especially the things attached to their once-cute feet, by the door, and not to just keep walking all through my house, up the stairs and then plop down on my bed. It's disgusting, and gross, and it feels like it is only the beginning of mud season and I have miles of floors to wash before I can rest and it's Just. Not. Fair.

I really do feel like a four-year-old ready to throw a big tantrum. It isn't fair that I have to be the one to clean up all their messes. This is not a complaint about my husband, because he does pitch in and help, though his version of help is usually getting the kids to do it, but hey, it's nice to not always be the person reminding the kids to clean up after themselves.

But still, it is never ending. Never, never, never ending.

I know they have busy little brains that are busy working on all the things they are working on and that figuring out how to do a cartwheel or ride their bike on the grass is taking all of their brain power, but I mean...

Mud.

Everywhere.

Absolutely everywhere in my house.

I just want to cry. But that would just mix with the dried mud on the floor that I just swept, I swear, and make more sticky mud.

Is that peanut butter on the stairs?

How did peanut butter fall on the stairs?

Food is not allowed in the upstairs of my house. Everyone knows this. This has been a long-standing rule, agreed upon by the two adults who live here.

There is chunky peanut butter on two of my steps.

I think I am going to cry now. I am out of paper towels at the moment, because hello, I am trying to be environmentally conscious and use washable rags as much as possible.

I don't want to pick up this peanut butter with my hands. None of my kids are claiming to be involved, and I seriously doubt the cat had anything to do with it.

Of course, my Dad would point out that if I had a dog I would never have found the peanut butter on the floor because the dog would have eaten it first. Completely ignoring the fact that a dog would mean four more feet to track more mud, dirt, ticks, and burrs into my house. Not to mention that dogs have gross bodily fluids like kids, and this cat at least seems happy to go potty outside when it's warm enough. And she buries her droppings, so it's not like I have to clean up after her like a dog.

Seriously – peanut butter on my stairs. I am sure each of my children has walked past it (managing somehow not to step on it – I am not sure how that's even possible) at least 20 times. Granted, the stairs are painted brown and peanut butter is tan, but these are girls I am raising – they are supposed to be good at picking out nuances. I mean, we evolved for the gathering portion of hunting and gathering, so really, it shouldn't still be there!

It means a separate trip for me. Because I almost never go up or down the stairs without having my hands full. I usually have a tote bag on my shoulder with my knitting, phone, tablet and book(s), and a drinking vessel in the other hand at the bare minimum. Plus I broke an ankle less than a year ago, so really, peanut butter on the stairs is a huge safety hazard.

Maybe they just think it looks like mud?

Maybe, as the comedian Dennis Leary once shared, it's like a PB & J sandwich that was flying around and needed a place to park. In the VHS player. Where you put a VHS tape.

Thank the Goddess I have never found anything parked in the DVD player. I think that's why we keep it sideways, so it doesn't look like a drawer of any kind.

But seriously, PB on the stairs?

KIDS VS. CHORES

This whole kids versus chores thing really sucks.

I can't run a household of six all on my own, and ever get to do *anything* else. Because you've met kids, right? They just drop, and smear, and drip, and leave mud everywhere, and who knows what other gross stuff, because sometimes it is just easier to clean it up than identify what it is.

Am I right?

You know I'm right.

It's gross and disgusting and thank God they are cute, because sometimes we really don't know why we keep cleaning up after them. And that's just the husbands! No, seriously, joking aside, we are all just a tiny bit messy (especially if you are at all creative, and that's like hardwired in our basic DNA over here). Mess happens. A lot. Like, constantly. If I want to have a life outside of being a cleaner (which by the way is nothing I would ever aspire to) then other people have to help.

Living in a state of chaos and filth is not an option. And I haven't quite figured out where in the budget to pay for the cleaner. I know I need to, but I am just not quite ready to cross that bridge yet. I think that will be a goal for next year.

In the meantime, there's shit that needs to be done around here and it's not all my stuff, and it's not all your stuff, some of it is communal stuff. You can say *put your dishes away* until you are blue in the face, but someone has to do the dishes that made the food, and it isn't exactly anybody's responsibility. Just saying. I in no way endorse slavery of any kind, but I can totally see the appeal some days, as a mother of four. I mean, I feel like one myself.

The truth is, we have to get stuff done, and kids need to learn to help. They are going to need these skills later to be humans that any other human would want to live with. I mean, I don't really want them to have mad sex skills in order to get to live somewhere, you know what I mean? I really hope not to know that much about their sex lives. I want them to be happy, but I really don't need to know about what's going on in anyone's bedroom as long as both people are happy and in a healthy relationship.

But I digress – because it is so hard to stay focused in all this kid clutter. They need to be the ones to pick some of this shit up and look after some of this stuff. My eldest is pretty good at looking after her ducks. She's not perfect, and we have to check on the whole food and water situation from time to time, but I would say she is good 85 percent of the time. Which is better than anyone else who needs tons of reminders, cajoling and *no you don't get to do that thing you wanted to do until the thing I asked you to do ten times already today is done.*

Yes, there are times when I would really so much rather just do the thing myself. Not because I enjoy doing it, but because the energy it takes to get someone else to do it is just too much. But if I don't, how are they going to learn? How are they going to get the things that need to get done, done? How is all this going to happen in a respectable way?

Because these things need to get done. Lately I have given up and said things like, "The bathrooms need to be cleaned and you all need to work out how that is happening. Everyone needs to participate and do some part of the job, but I really don't want or need to hear the details and y'all just need to get it done."

Strangely enough, that has been working. The bathroom has been getting clean, even the inside of the toilet bowl, which they hate. So now my bathroom is no longer a grotty mess. It's nice. It's a start.

Now if only dishes and laundry and picking up your shit was that easy.

But I guess then I would be out of a job as a mother, right? Retirement – that's when you don't have to pick up kid shit anymore, right? Because grandkids pick up after themselves, right? You bribe them with toys and candy and they just clean up because it's Grandma's house and Grandma's rules

Right? How do I get there again?

Oh, by keeping this generation alive.

Riiiight!

EATING WITH KIDS

Eating with your kids has got to be something that was created as a form of parental torture. Seriously. When they are little it is sort of easy. Whether from a boob or a bottle, it's just a sucking action with the occasional spit up and puke.

Unless, of course, you give birth to a puke-a-saurus like I did. She would be happily nursing along, then come off my nipple long enough to puke before then latching back on as if nothing had happened, and all the while I have puke dripping all down my front, my lap, and all the creases of my body. But she has just re-latched so I can't exactly pass her off to her Dad, right? That's what it felt like, anyway.

I remember for my first birthday after becoming a mother all I wanted was to not be puked, peed, or pooped on for one day. That didn't happen, but that was all I truly wanted for my birthday.

Since kids don't come out of the womb with table manners of any sort, it just goes downhill from there once you start letting them have anything that doesn't come in a bottle. You will soon find food everywhere, not just on your child, but in all these strange places you have never before seen food. Like, you know, flung on the walls or stuck to the underside of the table. Those of you with dogs may actually find less random food in random places since most dogs love babies for leaving treats everywhere. But considering the number of stories I have heard of dogs then puking and pooping all over the house, I am grateful that I usually only had one spewing creature at a time.

We are not going to get into sickness in this particular piece. Maybe later, but not now.

Even at ages 4, 6, 9 and 11, the table manners have not gotten super great. Yes, they use their knife and fork most of the time, but they still make really weird combinations of food on their plate, they don't eat everything, they leave food in random locations, and, well, sometimes I am just too tired to actually want to watch them eat or correct that grossness sitting across the table. Sometimes I am just too excited that they did in fact actually eat something that I prepared and served to mention that perhaps they should actually use their fork. I mean, they are over the age of six, after all.

As I have said before, breakfast should not be a meal where I have to be civil to anyone. Not so much because I haven't yet imbibed enough caffeine (though that has been the case in other years) but just because I really don't want to have to have a conversation with all these hangry individuals who are doing what the name of the meal implies, breaking their fast. Kids almost always wake up hungry. All that time sleeping and recharging and growing makes a person hungry, you know. Or so I vaguely remember.

So it's not like they are at their best at breakfast either. They don't even get the prop of coffee or tea – or lack thereof – as a reason why they are miserable sods. My youngest (no matter which one it has been, because they all have been at one time or the other) often holds the worst stubborn tantrums around breakfast, and honestly, if she would just eat some food everything would get better.

But no, it needs to be the right bowl, the right spoon, the right amount of milk to drown out her oatmeal, which she will not finish anyway. The milk, I mean. For a couple of years now, the oatmeal gets left on the table for a couple of hours after breakfast, not solely because we are slobs but also because my littles often come back for second or third breakfasts, like the true hobbits I apparently spawned.

It is just so gross. Even when they're not being gross you have to cut up their meat, dish them up seconds before you've had your first bite, and clean up their plates afterward (or not – but still cringe at what hit the trash or compost bucket). Or they have the nerve to try and steal your food – that last bite that you learn to take first, or just that one more bite you were hoping to have.

As if that's not enough, some days you miscalculate how much they are going to eat and you haven't made them enough food, and so you are so excited that they are eating at all that you give them some of yours, and by the time you are done you now have to scrounge around for more food yourself. Let's face it, that is never going to be a time where you make a good nutritional choice. Carbs and processed food are just way too easy to pop in your mouth when you have gotten to the overly hungry part of life.

Yep. Eating with kids is gross. Maybe by the time they are teenagers it will get better. I don't have my fingers crossed or anything though. I don't have boys, so there is a small possibility it might improve, right?

WHY CAN'T KIDS JUST CLEAN UP?

Why don't kids help clean up? Is this just an American thing? My friend whose son is half German has shown pictures of him neatly lining everything up, even his shoes under his bed. So some kids must want to live in a clean house where they put their toys away, right?

Not any of my kids, though. Not if they are left to their own devices. I know. I have watched. I have purposely not cleaned up after them or put away all their detritus, and it has stayed there for as long as I can stand it. We're talking weeks, months, or until they have completely forgotten that the thing even existed.

My eldest is currently sharing a room with my youngest and there is about seven years' age difference. In personality and the need to snuggle at night, they are perfectly matched, but of course their skills at being able to put things away are not at all matched.

We have just moved. We are having an open house in a couple of days. So every afternoon, after I am done working and shuttling kids to their activities, I have been organizing and cleaning up one room. Putting things away, dusting, making sure it looks like a room we would like our friends to visit. The artwork and photographs haven't gotten hung yet (mainly because I haven't found our hangers) but otherwise it is all good. All that is left is the kitchen and the yard at this point, and I have a friend coming to help me with the kitchen tonight.

My kids are done with me and the cleaning, unpacking, and organizing, though. They complain bitterly that I am doing it and not doing whatever it is they want me to do. They complain when I ask them to take more things upstairs or down to the basement, or get me the broom.

They do, however, love the room when it's finished, and talk about how pretty it is and how much better it looks. They then proceed to play in said room and not pick up after themselves.

I wouldn't mind as much if they took the reminders to clean up well. I get it – it's not a lot of fun to put your stuff away. It is even less fun when you have to put someone else's stuff away! Believe me!

Some days I am just too tired. Like I literally have nothing left, no energy to do any sewing, or knitting, or mending, absolutely nothing left and it's hard to pick up after my own self, let alone them. But most of the time I do pick up after me.

I wish I had a magic wand that would help convince them to pick up and put their stuff away. To put all the ingredients back in the fridge when they are done constructing their sandwich. To put all their dishes in the sink or dishwasher and put the serving dishes away too.

Some of my daughters have gotten really good at walking all the way downstairs at night to put their laundry down the chute into the basement. My other girls leave their laundry in the upstairs bathroom for days...

Once we get caught up on the laundry backlog, they are going to get to start washing their own laundry, because maybe that will stop them from constantly losing their laundry in the process as well. Maybe it will feel more fair all the way around.

But we have to get caught up on that laundry monster. With the party coming, it is going to have to wait. After the party, perhaps I'll make a big push to clean all the clothes and get them sorted and put away. We will just have to wait and see.

Are you one of those lucky moms whose kids naturally pick up after themselves? If you are, can you share your secret recipe, or magic wand? Is there a special vitamin I need to feed them? Is there a possibility that someday they might clean up after themselves?

Or are they doomed to be gross roommates in the future? I know they say creative people tend to live in chaos, but I can never tell if that's just because their brains got used to it or if they really are happier that way. I think I am happiest with a maid. We aren't quite at the point where we want to pay for one yet. But maybe I should look into one. They at least don't complain.

THE PHANTOM POOPER

We have a phantom pooper at my house.

I don't mean those lovely little packages your toddler or sweet pet leaves for you. We have totally had those. One of our cats used to have to be crated at night because otherwise he would poop in front of the back door every night and I was pregnant, so the hell with cleaning that up.

I don't have any very small people left in my house. I have two cats who are *well outside-and-only-use-the-litter-box-during-the-winter* trained.

My youngest is 5 and has been completely potty trained for a couple of years now. My middles are mostly out of overnight diapers except when they are sick.

So my hubby and I were not expecting *phantom poop*.

You know that poop that happened in the toilet and for some godforsaken reason was never flushed down?

That one. It ends up getting under the toilet paper if someone else comes along and uses the toilet and like never actually looks in the bowl.

And it just sits there, not smelling so nice, and just mellowing and waiting for a grown-up to come along and hit flush.

I know from the size of the snakes that it is not an adult who is doing it. I mean, we all forget things sometimes, or get interrupted *because mom's pooping on the toilet* it must be time for an emergency. Like. Right. Now.

No, I am not talking about those times. This has become a pattern, but we can't figure out which of the kids is doing it.

I suspect it may in fact be more than one.

The 5-year-old usually makes me wipe her butt, so I think it's pretty safe to say it's not her.

I have caught the 10-year-old having left the poop in the bowl and she is a bit space cadet-y lately thanks to those lovely hormones that decided to show up already.

My eldest has been known to be the skiddie monster of her undies. Which has the added bonus of no one else being willing to wear her undies, and in a household of four girls I suspect that's just a way to mark her territory.

And my 7-year-old, it might be her. She's pretty happy-go-lucky, so it's possible. Or not - it's really hard to tell.

It tends to just be one bathroom too, the downstairs one. Which is currently off limits, as we have week-old ducks in a box on the floor right now, because it is too cold to keep them in the basement and well, the cats might think at their current size they would be yummy snacks.

So it will be interesting to see if the phantom pooper shows up now that we are down to one bathroom for the next couple of weeks until we can move the heat lamp over the ducks higher and move them all into the bathtub.

I mean, I know it could be so much worse. At least the poop is in the toilet, right? Not smeared on the walls or just squatting in the corner. I am grateful that days like that are behind us.

Which does beg the question of why this is even happening. At ages 5 to 12 you would think they would all be good in the bathroom department, right?

Everyone seems to have gotten over the *being scared of the flushing toilet sound.*

Or have they?

Maybe that's the problem....

It's too noisy?

Do you have a phantom pooper in your house? I'd love to hear about it if you do, so I know I am not the only one!

RANTS

Why Won't My Kids Get Dressed?

Some days getting my kids dressed is a full-blown mission. At ages 11, 9, 6 and 4 you would think it wouldn't be that hard. I know, perhaps if I sent them to school it would be easier because they would have to get dressed first thing in the morning every day. But honestly, between play-dates, errands, and Girl Scouts, they already have to get dressed on a regular basis most days.

I don't know if it's because it's the middle of winter and we had a cold winter to start with, or what exactly it is, but lately none of them want to get dressed in the morning, or at all. While honestly I really don't care – I mean, at least pajamas cover all the important bits – lately I have found that the more they are in pajamas, the more they fight, and complain about not feeling well, and give me the world's biggest sighs about doing the few chores we ask them to do around the house. Just general prickliness. I think that asking them to get dressed, to make an effort to put more than one layer of clothes on, would really help improve our day-to-day living.

They, however, could care less. Because I structure my day to get my client work done in the morning when at all possible, they are able to get away with not getting dressed until probably lunch time. I mean, who really wants to fight with them about clothes? They have too many fucking clothes as it is and they are strewn all over my house, their bedrooms, and are constantly in a state of needing to be washed or folded.

My hubby and I are super close to only letting them have three outfits for summer clothes this year because we are so tired of seeing the same clothes ending up in the to-be-washed pile, even though they haven't actually been on a daughter's body. Nope, they haven't been worn at all, and yet there they are needing to be washed again because someone dropped them on the floor and walked on them, and no one really wants to be wearing stepped-on clothes, do they?

But seriously, what is it about not getting dressed? They would be warmer and less irritable if they had more layers on. Because we heat our house with fuel oil, it is never going to be that warm in the winter. Maybe if we used wood or solar power or something it would be, but as long as we are burning dead dinosaurs I am not turning the heat up. Sorry, you each have about a dozen sweatshirts, sweaters, and jackets, so you really could just put another layer on. Not to mention that everyone has multiple pairs of thermals. So, seriously.

Recently all my hubby's socks have gone missing. I know I am supposed to care, because, you know, everyone should have socks. But since handing the laundry over to my 9-year-old I have tried as much as possible to stay out of the whole laundry thing. But I think I am going to have to go hunting for socks for him this week. I don't know where the hold-up is - if they are not actually getting washed, or if they are not getting folded. Because my girls seem to think that they can ignore the rags, socks, and handkerchiefs at the bottom of the laundry baskets until they fill half the basket and I complain - I mean, point out - that they really should be folding and putting away those items as well.

By and large my hubby has socks all the same color so it's not really a matter of trying to match up different pairs of socks. Of course, it is possible that there is a stash somewhere in our room of socks that never made it to be washed in the first place. I will be looking for that stash, rather than focusing on other areas where the socks might be. Other locations that they could be hiding sound like something the laundry processor and my husband need to deal with. Now if I can find where they haven't been washed then that part of the problem could be solved by an adult. Potentially.

But seriously, why not get dressed? You have plenty of clothes. You would think the duck-loving girl would get dressed before going out to see her ducks, but since it is cold enough to warrant snow pants, she just puts her snow gear on top of her pajamas and away she goes, never actually bothering to get dressed. What's more, she is happily dressed quite early on weekends. There just seems to be something about weekdays when I am the only parent home, and where more often than not we do actually have someplace we need to be, when they all refuse to get dressed.

I have even tried saying I won't make lunch until people get dressed, but that ends up just becoming the world's biggest shit storm of unhappy girls and hangry people. I don't try that threat anymore. They do get dressed right before we walk out the door, but I feel like a lot of the angst and squabbling could be avoided if only they would get dressed!!!

FUCKING PUMPKIN SPICE

I happen to love pumpkin. I always have and I always will. My parents used to tease me and say I liked all things orange – pumpkin, sweet potatoes, oranges – because they matched my red hair. I don't know if that was true or not, I just know that those are some of my favorite foods.

There is even a story that at almost 11 months old, for my first Thanksgiving I managed to eat a full portion of everything and even a full slice of pumpkin pie.

So it's kinda my thing. One of my Mom's favorite recipes has always been a pumpkin quick bread, because it makes two loaves so you can take one to a potluck and still have one to eat at home. Full of pumpkin, spices, walnuts, and raisins – what's not to love?

My mom canned pumpkin too, so we always had it around. I think we even used to make pumpkin cookies sometimes.

So in my twenties, when the first pumpkin lattes came out, I used to get them when we would visit Barnes & Noble and the Starbucks inside. I know lots of people are anti-Starbucks, but this was the early

2000s, and back in those days they were one of the few coffee shops that had a dairy milk alternative. Being married to someone allergic to dairy, it did determine where we shopped to buy coffee (and still does). Starbucks is one of the few places that has coconut milk, as my hubby doesn't like what happens to almond milk in coffee, and let's face it, soymilk is not that good for you to drink if you're male.

It was pretty good in the beginning, before it was everywhere. Like I said, I happen to like pumpkin.

However, almost two decades later, um, I could care less. We happened to be in a city recently and therefore stopped at Starbucks. We get our coffee from nice local shops whenever we can, but have yet to find them in Augusta. I ordered a lightly-sweetened (don't add any sugar at all, please) chai. I was really surprised at how pumpkin-y it tasted. Like, really, if you added some whipped cream and sprinkled nutmeg on top, it could have totally been a pumpkin spice latte.

Which wasn't what I was going for. No, I wanted a chai. It's not the same thing. Chai has peppercorns and turmeric. Yes, it also has cloves, ginger, and cinnamon, but the peppercorns and turmeric change the taste quite a lot. Oh, and cardamom - a good chai needs that as well, and that definitely keeps it out of the pumpkin pie realm.

I still love pumpkin pie and I make a couple for Thanksgiving. We often eat it for breakfast, because who wants to cook breakfast with everything else on Thanksgiving? I still eat pumpkin. It doesn't need any sweetener, in my opinion. I even put it in my smoothies to change things up.

But I don't need it in fucking everything.

I don't need all the back-to-school, back-to-fall advertising to be only about pumpkin spice. Let's face it, there is so much more to fall than just pumpkin.

There are so many other lovely winter squashes to enjoy and appreciate. Change them up and get some other great vitamins.

Not that a pumpkin latte is actually providing you with anything of nutritional value. Not if you are buying it. If you are making it, possibly, depending on the sugar and dairy you are using. But the stuff you buy at a store.... pumpkin flavored coffee and most beers do not have any pumpkin in them! I mean, what's the point? Why not just say cinnamon spice coffee and beers? Why call it pumpkin when you aren't even using it?

And don't get me started on Jack-o-Lanterns. Just don't.

IT IS OKAY TO SAY NO

It really is. It is okay to use a no-nonsense or stern tone of voice. To not put a question like *okay?* at the end of your sentence.

It is okay to create boundaries: around acceptable behavior, around what is okay and not okay in your family, around being alone in the bathroom, around chores, around life.

It is okay to raise your kids to the best of your ability, your way, and not necessarily the way the rest of the world tells you that you should.

It's okay to say no to sugar, to say yes to sugar, to let your kids stay up late, to put them to bed early, and to let them have a sleepover on a school night, if that is what works for you and your family.

It's okay to try something and discover that it doesn't work for your family and then forget and try it again later and still discover that it's a really bad idea.

It's okay to use your partner as the bad guy when you say no to a social event, even if they really don't care.

It's okay to not give your kids choices about everything. To say this is what is for lunch and you can either eat it or not. It's okay to not give them a plethora of clothing and to take them to the library regularly rather than buying them lots of books.

It's okay to let them watch TV when you really need to make that uninterrupted phone call or just have five minutes of peace before you lose your shit.

It's okay to have the tooth fairy forget to deliver and have to come the next night. It's a great chance to practice your creative storytelling as to why the tooth fairy forgot.

It's okay to eat breakfast for dinner or spend a day just eating peanut butter if that's the best that you can do that day.

It is okay to feel guilty and wonder if you are a good mother, because in stopping to wonder you have a chance to become a better mother, rather than just assuming that you do in fact suck.

It's okay to suck.

We all suck at being mothers sometimes. And that's okay because our kids are going to suck at being parents sometimes too, and at least this way we are modeling realistic examples.

It's okay to need to apologize. It's okay to need to apologize a lot.

Because you are growing, just like your family.

It's okay to get mad

And angry and frustrated and so fucking tired you can't see straight.

It's okay to need to take a few minutes away from your kids, even though parenting is all you have ever wanted to do and you truly believe it is the best job ever. It's okay to need a break and to walk away.

It's okay to ask for help. It's okay to have a village help take care of your family.

It's okay to say no not just to your kids but to the world and to do your best to just do the things you want to do.

It's okay to just be the best person you can be. Because in the end, that will make you the best parent for your child. Because they are unique and so are you, and your uniqueness just might help them discover and empower their own.

It's okay to say no.

WHY CAN'T WE HAVE ALL THE THINGS?

We parents are constantly telling our kids no. No you can't have that toy, no you can't have more candy (because if there is one more sugar crash today I am going to seriously lose my shit), no you can't go to that play date because you're double booked.

But if you do any work in abundance, you know that it's not about saying no to everything. It is about strategically saying yes to some things, and being open to what the Universe has to offer you, and hopefully what will make space for more abundance.

More yeses to the things. Maybe not actual things. Maybe experiences, maybe trainings, or maybe saying yes to staying in bed. Or stopping what you are doing and playing with the kids for a while.

Maybe it's saying yes to being silly for a few moments. Or having fun.

Or saying yes to binge-watching some movies, or cleaning out clutter from drawers. Maybe it's saying yes to new possibilities.

But we can't really say yes to everything we want, can we? We are told the world has finite resources (though of course we are constantly teaching our children that our love is infinite), so we can't use up all the stuff.

Sometimes we don't actually want all the stuff. We just want some of the things. Some of the everyday things.

We want them. But sometimes when you have to delay that gratification (which according to the marshmallow study means you will be happier later in life) you end up not really being that excited for it when it finally arrives. At least if it's stuff. If it's not an experience. I have yet to be disappointed that it's time to go on vacation. Come home maybe, but actually take the time off, no, that's usually good.

I don't get sad just because the weekend is starting, those things are really good.

But is the drive for all the things actually a drive for companionship, support, a cry for help that our needs aren't been met? Or is it just that we need that thing, whatever it is?

Maybe it's just really super good marketing. I have been around marketing for so long that I totally notice that when it's for good stuff, when the marketing is cutting-edge, or really well done, that it actually gets me. I notice those things. I truly do.

What if the craving for all the things is just marketing? Can we turn all that off? Can we unsubscribe from all the emails and catalogues? Can we only go to shop when we actually need something and then put our blinders up? Can we ignore the ads on social media? Can we manage to not look up the latest and greatest shiny object?

Can we get a cool idea and then look at what we have around us and see if we can build it with what we already have? Or adjust it slightly? Or just make it a tiny bit better? Can we do any of that?

Can we teach our kids that if you want it badly enough you can have it, but to be super clear if that's the thing they truly want?

Can we help them deal with the disappointment of saving up for something they really wanted only to be sad that it wasn't quite what they thought it was, or that it is harder to do, or that they actually lost interest in owning it while they were saving for it but were still in love with the idea?

Can we help them understand that it's love and companionship and at times just being alone that makes life worth living? That the challenge is what their brain is craving, is what gives them the dopamine hit and not owning the actual thing? That disappointment is normal on birthdays and Christmas and other gift-giving holidays, and it is the anticipation that the brain is going for? That the sweet anticipation is what we all want?

How do we teach this to kids? How do we show them that wanting to have all the things is probably not about having all the things, but having the big fundamental desires, like a roof over their head, and yummy food to eat, and time with parents and friends, and games to play. That is what they are truly craving, not actually all the things.

PARENT TORTURE: READING ALOUD FROM GRAPHIC NOVELS

There is a new section in the children's area of the library. Have you found it yet? It's small in some libraries and quite large in others. It seems to magically draw any child over the age of three, and certainly any child who has a grasp of what books are, what they are for, and their ABCs.

It can be a dangerous section, depending on your library and whether they separate the middle school years from the high school years for these types of books. While I am okay with kids reading beyond where they are ready, especially where books are concerned, the fact that these books are so heavily illustrated leaves a lot less to the imagination.

I get that graphic novels – this new type of book that is really just a much longer version of the comic books we grew up with – are helpful for certain types of emerging readers. They can help bridge that gap between the visual of the drawings and the written word. So much of the storytelling is revealed by the illustrations in panels rather than just the words.

They're a great crossover, providing your child has a good grasp on the level of reading that a particular graphic novel requires.

But if they don't – if the reading is beyond them, or they found a sibling's copy and they can't read it yet themselves – well, that can lead to you having to help them.

I don't mind helping with an occasional word, or even sitting there while they sound out the words and read it aloud to me.

But when I have to read a graphic novel out loud, I just want to tear my hair out. Literally, can I do *anything* else for you right now, like scrub a toilet? Clean up vomit? Walk the dog? Anything?

Because it is so hard to read a graphic novel aloud. There are so many made-up words that are just sounds that for some reason have to be shown as letters and are way more complicated than just *pfft*. It can be hard to know if your child is ready to move on from that panel, much less that page, in a timely manner, because the illustrations can be so deep.

There are often no chapters or other obvious stopping points, so you could be stuck reading the whole book from front to back in one sitting, even though they are usually well over 100 pages.

If you are the type of parent who skims over the truly gross, cruel, or violent portions of books when you are reading them aloud to your young children, that really cannot be done in graphic novels. Your child is going to know that something bad or evil is going on just by the drawings, not to mention the words. By and large, graphic novels take from their comic book roots and there is a lot more violence than your average middle school aged book.

And it's not like they come with a rating system! They aren't rated with reading difficulty or violence level or even liberal vs. conservative viewpoints. I homeschool my kids so that stuff doesn't bother me as much because my kids will talk to me about what we are reading, what they have been reading, and we will discuss things (because even their Readers books have occasionally had things in them we have had to discuss).

It's probably no worse than the same kind of TV show. I keep my kids on pretty tight reins for what they can watch on TV, and they are girls, so they aren't even interested in watching Power Rangers or Clone Wars (though they are amazingly quite fond of Dino Trucks and Troll Hunters), so I am not sure what the current violence levels in those shows are.

I totally understand the draw of graphic novels, especially when you are bridging from picture books into chapter books without pictures. But they are so hard to read aloud, to share with another person at the same time. You can totally read it, and then have someone else read it and discuss it, but the act of enjoying them simultaneously, well, maybe I am just not wired to do that.

Oh and I should throw out there that they are usually soft-sided paperback books of weird shapes and sizes, which can make finding them and keeping tabs on them when they have been borrowed from the library a bit of at trick at times. Believe me, you would rather not have to buy a missing graphic novel from the library, because when you eventually find it again, it will now be your copy and that means you might get asked to read it aloud...*again*.

WHY DO WE BASH EACH OTHER ON WHAT WE READ OR WATCH?

Why is there even the concept of a guilty pleasure or trashy television?

Why do we think that the only books worth reading are the ones that have to have some literary value, when at the end of the day we really just want five minutes to have a semi-adult thought?

Why do we judge other mothers for watching a drama in the middle of the day when they could be spending that time with their kids?

Why do we all hide the fact that we read *50 Shades of Grey* or watched the movies?

Even though at times we are loath to admit that we have watched or read these things, we are also quite happy to post on social media asking for a new show to binge-watch the next time we get a chance.

Dealing with kids all day every day is hard, whether you are a working mom, a stay-at-home mom or a working-from-home mom. Whether your kids are in school or stay home with you, being a mom is hard.

And boring.

A lot of parenting is infinitely boring. The number of hours I have spent in a bathroom with small children using the toilet...

Hours processing dishes.

Folding laundry.

Wiping down surfaces after sticky hands and muddy feet and doing general picking up.

The number of hours I have had to listen to inane preschool programming on the television, or watch my child play a stupid app game.

Or had my music choices dictated by someone under five feet tall.

It is enough to feel as though your brain has gone to mush.

Literal mush.

You would like to have an intelligent conversation.

You would like to feel like you have some idea of what is going on in the big wide world outside of your little person's head.

You don't have time to figure out if news is fake or not. You're lucky if you can find five minutes to scroll through your social media feed.

So getting to watch anything that is not a kid show, or getting to read anything that doesn't fucking rhyme, for fuck's sake, is a miracle.

A delightful miracle. Those things become your lifeline.

It's your chance, for a few moments, to feel like there might be more to life than just cleaning up sticky faces. That other people have thoughts and ideas and maybe, just maybe, their life is far more screwed up than yours.

So I say have your guilty pleasure when you can. Read a steamy romance, or heck, sign up for Audible's monthly *all the romance you can listen to* membership.

Watch the drama-filled TV show (maybe not around the kids, unless you want to have to answer an incescent number of questions). Perhaps take 30 minutes to put your feet up and read a book. Or hide out in the bathroom reading a book.

These are all beautiful things and we should share what we found that helped us get through the day. Even if they are what others might find trashy and look down their nose at. Because they worked for us, and in the end, that is what matters. They worked for us and helped us come back more engaged with our kids the next time around.

SHE'S TOUCHING ME!

She is sitting next to me.

At least at this moment she is not insisting on lifting up my shirt and touching my "mole-ys" that have become her points of comfort since being weaned.

But she is still sitting next to me while I try to work and get things done.

She is playing on her Kindle and talking, and expecting me to be able to keep up with both her game and her chatter. I am busy actually writing and working and doing my best not to pay attention to her at all, so I can get my work done.

But she is only 4-and-a-half.

And she has been sick lately. We all have, with a 48-hour fever and then the rest of the cold symptoms that last for a few days afterward. When you are a family of six, in my experience, illness doesn't move as rapidly through everyone. Which is nice because you do not have six people down at once, but it can also seem never-ending, because once two or three of us have gotten sick it's hard to remember that we haven't all gotten it yet.

At least it is better than the summer they had chicken pox, which was annoying in that it was the summer and we were stuck inside for weeks. But it was good because they all got it at once – okay really one got it and then about 10 days later the other three got it in the space of 72 hours – and it's one of those things I wanted them to get and then let us move on.

Politics of vaccinations aside, this is what most of us went through as kids and honestly they haven't gotten super sick since we did that almost two summers ago.

But she is still sitting there giggling, and playing, and needing to be close to me.

Just as much as I need to work on my laptop in my pajamas in bed today, because I am too tired and sick to want to get dressed yet.

I will, because I have places to be and things I have to do later in the day-to-day. But one advantage to working from home is that I don't have to get dressed at a certain time most days.

My clients can't see me.

Since most of them work from home as well, for all I know they are in their pajamas too. I do get dressed most of the time. It takes being really sick for me not to get dressed. I plan on getting dressed after I finish up my work for today. I'll go take a shower (because that should allow me to hide from the girls for a while and I need that more than the getting clean part) and then get dressed and then go downstairs and read our chapter book aloud. I was supposed to do it at breakfast, but one of my girls who is of course still sick hadn't gotten up yet, so we had to save it for later.

I am hoping to finish this read-aloud book with them soon. It's a good story, and the book is under 300 pages, but for whatever reason it is taking a long time to get it read to them. I suspect it is because they love Harry Potter more and if given the choice and we can only read one, they want Potter. It's *The Order of the Phoenix* so it may never get finished. Four-hundred-plus pages in and we would have already finished the first two or three books, but we aren't even halfway done with *Phoenix*. Oh well, the things we do for the love of our kids.

Like letting them sit next to us when they are sick, even though the giggles and chatter are slightly annoying. Mainly because I am not firing on all cylinders myself, but also because it's just so hard to follow sometimes. The mind of a 4-year-old is so far removed from that of a 38-year-old that sometimes it is hard to follow what she is saying

But hopefully she will have some vague memories of sitting next to me.

Or of the love. Or of holding mole-ys.

Or she'll just remember to do it for her kids.

That makes it worthwhile, right?

That and knowing that I can hide in the shower in a few minutes.

SHOPPING WITH KIDS

My 4-year-old had been acting better on shopping trips lately. The "I wants" had not been coming out and she had been reasonably patient and helpful during the last few shopping trips.

So I had forgotten.

Forgotten how difficult it can be to go shopping with children.

On Tuesday I needed to go to the dollar store to buy some band-aids and other first aid supplies for our Daisy Girl Scout meeting that night. I took all four of my kids because it was the middle of the day and I had promised my 6-year-old that she could pick out the bandaids for her troop because they have some pretty ones at the dollar store.

I also brought everyone because I wanted to stock up on snacks for while we are moving, both to just be able to shove food at the kids and also so they had food to bring with them when they were hanging out at friends' houses. Since I am unable to remember who likes what anymore (because I swear they keep changing their minds!) I brought everyone along.

My first warning sign should have been that she wasn't initially willing to get in the cart. Also, it was super difficult for her to deal with the fact that her sister was going to be looking for a birthday present that we needed to put together for a friend of ours.

It pretty much went downhill from there. There was a lot of kicking out of her feet which didn't make me want to push her in the cart.

There were a lot of demands about where she wanted to be pushed next, and lots of holding on to things that she wanted to buy. As it was the dollar store, I was more than willing to buy her a set of bubble makers in the shape of popsicles to share with her sisters at the new house.

Of course, it didn't help that some of her sisters couldn't really find snacks that they wanted, or took forever to decide. Even though they had eaten lunch, apparently they had gotten hungry again on the 20-minute car ride, or more accurately all the food marketing and packaging was making them hungry and whiny.

We finally checked out and made it out of the store, but we still needed to go to Walmart to buy the rest of our groceries.

Yes, I said it, Walmart, and don't you go getting all judgy with me. I do my best to shop as local and USA-made as I can, but when it comes down to the basics of food, there are times where you really do need to stretch your dollar. Believe it or not, there are also times that in my neighborhood Walmart has the nicer produce, and they sell organic just like the grocery stores do. In my area, there are currently no locally-owned grocery stores, so does it matter if I am going to Walmart, Shaws, or Hannaford? They are all big box stores.

By shopping where I can stretch my dollar I am able to do more local shopping as well. Just saying that it can in fact work both ways!

Anyway, by the time we get to Walmart and have a bathroom stop (in the back in the family bathroom because they have the mini toilets that just make my 4-year-old so happy) we hit up the craft kit aisle (not in the toy department, in the craft department, I am not that crazy) to pick out the final couple of pieces for the birthday gift we are putting together.

Unfortunately my 4-year-old sees the paint-your-own ceramic Elsa from Frozen piggy bank. And she wants one. I can understand why. It's tall, it looks cool, and it's nice and breakable. What more could a 4-year-old want?

The only problem is that 1) I am not shopping for my daughter at the moment and it is way too far out to get her something for her birthday that she knows about, 2) my husband is the only one with the painting skills to make this bank look recognizably like Elsa and 3) we still need to get a craft kit for the person we came into this aisle for in the first place.

But we have deeply triggered the "I wants," which currently come out in the words "please, please, please," said over and over again to my consistent "no's." I guess I am lucky that she doesn't try to bargain yet.

We finally make it out of the aisle with what we need and even while I am pushing the cart down to the grocery section she is still asking about it. She wants me to buy her anything really at this point and I am still standing firm in my no. I am internally reminding myself how I usually try and set my children up for success and not failure while shopping and wondering where I went wrong this time around.

We finally make it to check out and I prepare to pay and the register decides to stop working and completely deletes my transaction and the cashier is new and doesn't seem to understand the urgency when it comes to getting the manager to help.

Finally we check out again with the manager, who is amazing and keeps my girls engaged while she uses the wand to rescan all our items except for the few that need to be weighed, and we finally make it out to the car.

Where my 4-year-old no longer wants to get buckled in her car seat. No amount of cajoling seems to work. While I try to take a few minutes to help her identify her feelings, in the end I just sit patiently in the driver's seat until she finally gives up and gets hooked.

I vow to myself that I am not taking her shopping again for at least another month. Because this was just too hard.

And I am too tired and old to put up with this shit.

Frankly, who needs to go shopping anyway? I need to see if any of the CSAs will still let me sign up and find out how much Amazon can deliver to my door, because I am *done* shopping with my kids for a while!

You hear me? Done!

DRIVING

Driving.
I'm always driving.
Constantly
Stuck behind
This
Wheel.
The road rarely
Changes
Only the stories
In our heads
And the words
Left unsaid.
Driving.
I'm always
Driving.
Never
Arriving
Or leaving
Just driving.
And if it's about the
Journey
And not
The destination at the
End
Then what
The
Hell
Am I doing
Again?
Driving.
Always
Driving
Without
End.

BACK TO SCHOOL

What message are we sending about *Back to School*?

It's that time of year again. The one I hate the most. The one that seems over the top with consumerism – especially aimed at mothers.

No, I am not talking about Mother's Day. Nor Valentine's Day. Not your anniversary, Christmas, or even Easter and Halloween.

I am talking about *Back to School*. Which these days seems to be an excuse to bring out the pumpkin spice lattes, but I digress.

All the *Back to School* marketing seems to start like magic in the last week of July. Because, you know, some schools start in the middle of August. I live in Maine, where most schools start the day after Labor Day. Maybe the week before if they are worried about impending snow days, but here it's usually a post-Labor-Day thing.

But you wouldn't get that if you walked into any major chain store or have been on social media. The first day of school photos are coming.

Sigh. I don't do first day of school photos because my kiddos are homeschooled. Some of my other homeschooling friends still do their first day of homeschool photos. I silently vomit in my mouth. Because yes, while it is fun to see how much your kids have grown in the last 9 months, at the other end we have to see all the compilations of first and last day of school photos. Which really are not that much better than the school photos we had to sit for in the 80s and 90s. We are not all naturally better photographers and most of the time at least one of our kids doesn't even really want to pose. It's pretty obvious after a certain age that they are just doing this for their parents.

You know, there are plenty of other occasions to take photos of your kids, like birthdays and pumpkin patches and seasonal outside activities, if you need to see how much your kiddo has grown. You don't need to celebrate sending them away from you for a minimum of nine hours a day.

That is the message all that *Back to School* hype is celebrating. We are celebrating that we get to send our kids away from us. That we get to get rid of them. That they are going away, because we as moms couldn't possibly stand to be around our kids all day once they are over the age of five. Like it would seriously kill us or something.

Now you know me, I am all for every parent getting regular breaks from their children. Keeping those little people alive takes a lot of energy, and everyone needs the opportunity to have an adult conversation from time to time. Seriously, we do. And I think you should get as many breaks as you can in a way that works for you and your children.

But saying that I need my kids gone nine hours a day, five days a week for nine months out of the year to be a sane adult is selling me and my kids short. Now I am not going to get into the "I need to work full time outside of my home" conversation because I am all for women's rights and if that is what is best for you and your family, go for it. I am all for stay-at-home dads, too, and for the first four years of my parenting journey my hubby was the stay-at-home parent.

But why do we need to celebrate sending our kids to an institution? Are we really looking forward to the fights over homework? The schlepping them to all the after school activities? Dealing with bullying and *so-and-so doesn't like me anymore?* Are we really looking forward to sick days and having to explain why our kids have to do this stupid piece of make-work homework that we know isn't going to teach them any valuable skills? Are we really looking forward to the parent-teacher meetings and feeling like we are being judged on the ability of our kids to survive school?

Are we really ready for the PTA meetings and our judgment of the other students and parents?

Are we really creating an environment in which our kids can succeed? Do you really find making your kids' school lunches (or paying for them) exciting?

Do you really hate being with your kids 24/7? Because that is the message we are sending them with all the hype about going back to school. Not to mention all the unnecessary shopping. I was in a *Bed Bath and Beyond* – in July, mind you - and they had sheets up of what everyone needed for all the local college dorms! So apparently you don't get off the hook even when your kids are going off to college. In my day we hit up thrift shops and got hand-me-down towels from retirees who were downsizing.

Do you really want to buy into celebrating the end of summer? Regardless of your feelings about fucking pumpkin spice?

SUGAR MONSTERS

I really think I should ban sugar.

For reals. Because the sugar crashes my kids have are going to be the death of me.

I'm not kidding.

The yelling and screaming and the inability to be anything but miserable when they come off that sugar high, followed by the wheedling, scheming, and whining to get more sugar.

I am done. The sugar monsters need to leave my house and never come back. They can take their sugar-saturated fruit with them. I would rather my kids eat veggies any day than pig out on bananas, oranges, pineapple, etc.

I am taking a stand and becoming one of THOSE moms. One who doesn't let their kids OD on candy. Not that your kids can't. I have let my kids do it and personally I don't want to pay those consequences any more. But that's just me. Feel free to do you.

This past weekend was Easter. While we don't celebrate, we do often get together for a shared meal with a local family and often egg-dyeing and possibly an Easter Egg hunt come along with it. Last year we hid glass beads and then the kids spent a good hour trading the beads and starting to string them. My eldest made several earrings out of them. I really liked the idea of non-candy-filled plastic eggs and even volunteered to help fill them.

But this time another mum took up the mantle of filling the eggs, since she was not contributing very many dishes to the meal. Originally she said that only about 40 percent of the eggs were filled with candy, which I didn't know until after we got there. I really didn't want my kids eating more sugar than they had already consumed in her lovely fruit salad.

I really appreciated that she was contributing in the best way that she knew. But I didn't realize that I would be bringing kids home who not only had a severe case of the sugar monsters, but also decided to be fully enthralled in the several balloons they had gotten along with stickers in the few eggs they had found that didn't contain candy.

I am not awesome at tying latex balloons shut. I have had to learn as a parent, because you know, this is what you have to do. So when they decided yesterday afternoon that the balloons were not big enough, or needed to be undone so they could play with them in the bath, I really, really wanted to lose my shit. Seriously. Because you know, sugar monsters – and crazy life stuff going on as well, because you know your kids don't become sugar monsters and make balloon untying demands on a normal day.

They have radar against that, you know, like how they all come out of the woodwork the moment the phone rings, or you decide to take a bath.

It must be something written on their chromosomes.

But back to what I was saying. No more sugar. Because the sugar monsters are the worst. I have totally used candy or cookies as bribery, in a controlled manner. There was a while where I was paying my kids their Halloween candy in exchange for chores. It worked remarkably well until everyone's favorite kind had run out, and my house looked better than it unfortunately normally does.

But the crashes. Albeit they are a bit easier to deal with when it is the time of year where you can just throw them outside, or take them to the playground. But lately my youngest really truly becomes a monster, my 6-year-old dissolves in a puddle of tears over the smallest thing, my 9-year-old gets nasty, and my 11-year-old has the biggest breakouts on her poor face.

So I am done. No more candy, no more brownies. Thank God we don't have any birthday parties to attend for a couple of weeks.

Because I am too tired for this shit.

Much, much too tired.

WHY WON'T THEY GO THE FUCK TO SLEEP?

I mean, seriously. What is it about children that they seem to never, and I mean never, feel the need to sleep when it is dark outside? I mean, sure, they are good at sleeping randomly in the middle of the afternoon or on car rides, when you're not planning on them sleeping. They seem to have the ability to take a nap whenever.

But at night, when you want to sleep, that seems to be a completely different thing. One they can't seem to manage. I have four kids and two of them have been good sleepers since infancy and two of them, not so much.

Right now (and I am not trying to make any changes because we are in the middle of moving) my girls all go up to bed at the same time each night, usually around 8:30. We don't do nightly baths and we don't necessarily read bedtime stories (though we have been reading Harry Potter aloud for a while now and we are still 150 pages away from finishing the *Order of the Phoenix*). We just say goodnight and send them upstairs. Yes, it then takes them half an hour to brush their teeth and do whatever else they have decided they need to do before going to bed, and some nights we have to get involved and remind them.

Some nights they come back down the stairs multiple times, though in the last few nights it has only been once or twice. But they still need to come down at least once.

My almost–12–year–old is dealing with the stress of homebuying by starting out the night in her bed and then moving to a nest she has made on the floor at the bottom of our bed around about one o'clock in the morning. Most of the time my husband and I sleep through it, and apparently she does as well, because she often seems confused as to how she got there the next morning.

My youngest likes to stall the longest about actually getting into her bed, though most of the time she seems to fall asleep reasonably quickly. She most certainly likes to dictate the stories they tell each other, or the songs they sing, or whatever the fuck else they do before actually surrendering to sleep.

My middle two daughters are sleeping in more lately, which is fine since we are homeschoolers. I really don't care that much. It only becomes problematic if my eldest thinks we should read Harry Potter at breakfast and I refuse to read it if not everyone is up. I also refuse to allow her to wake her sisters up.

I know all of this is going to change soon. We are going to move from a three bedroom house to a four bedroom house with dedicated office space for me to use in the morning while they are still probably sleeping. They will have more space in the two bedrooms they get, and there is always an adjustment period while everything finishes getting moved in and we finish unpacking. Since we have a full basement I am hoping most of the boxes can go in the basement and that way we don't feel like all of the new house is in chaos as we unpack one box at a time and put things away.

I am also deluding myself that this will mean that I will be able to sort and put away the diaspora that has happened after living for four years in this house and that I will be able to put like with like more easily. That and 12 closets should help a lot.

Yesterday morning I started nodding off while waiting for my computer to do a massive update. I had already gone on a two-mile walk in the brisk morning air, but I was more than ready to shut my eyes for a little while. This may be because my coping mechanism in times of stress is to sleep as much as I can when I can't do anything else. Or it could just be because I am a mother of four children, one of whom moves into our bedroom every night, which is bound to be disturbing my sleep on some level.

However, my kids kept coming to talk to me about this, that, or the other thing, so finally I had to give up on the whole being able to doze any more. I envy old people who can just drift off and then wake back up again, over and over. As a mother, that sounds like a luxurious vacation to me.

To have a day of just dozing. I don't think it will happen in the next decade, because heaven forbid my kids manage to feed themselves for a few hours, but it is nice to dream about, and hope for.

Of course by that time my sleep will have been disrupted for so long I won't actually know what it looks like to have a normal sleep pattern, and that will be that.

But maybe I should just try and sneak in a bit more sleep during this time of stress. I often feel like that adage "sleep when the baby sleeps," while helpful and unhelpful (because occasionally you want to have a few waking moments without the baby) should be true even when your babies are long and full of elbows and knees and are no longer babies. You should sleep when they sleep.

We should declare days off to just be *lie in your bed and doze* days. You can read a book or color in your coloring book, but let your Dad and I get some sleep. We do carve out mornings and afternoons like this. It usually only happens undisturbed because we threaten to be having sex, which is true sometimes, but more often than not we are simply catching up on sleep, because that is actually what we need more sometimes.

But seriously, why the fuck won't kids just go to sleep?

PUT YOUR OWN FUCKING OXYGEN MASK ON FIRST

HIDING FROM MY KIDS

I love my kids. Obviously. You kinda have to love your kids to put up with them and live with them and clean up all their bodily fluids. I know some mothers can end up having a hard time bonding with their kids, and by and large I did not have that experience. I do truly love my kids. But just like I truly love my husband, that doesn't mean I want to be with them all the time, or every second of every day, because that will just drive me crazy.

For years I thought this need to hide or get away from my kids meant a) I was a bad mother and b) that I must be an introvert – and what the hell was an introvert doing with four kids? Yes, I have friends who have more or less kids, but four appears to be that borderline between having a small family and having a large one. Once you hit four or more kids, you're a large family and not usually included in family pricing.

Anyway, back to the introvert thing. I am not sure how true it is anymore. Do I need human interaction to be happy and survive? To an extent. Am I happy staying home for days on end lost in my own worlds of being in nature, crafting, or reading books? Absolutely.

I grew up in a household of introverts, so the examples of behavior I saw were all of that nature. But I am not sure that makes me an introvert. I think maybe I am just someone who can adapt to either situation.

I think most people need to be able to survive without someone with them 24/7, but then again, I share a bed with my husband, so maybe we aren't supposed to? That's what I tell my kids when they complain about sharing a room.

Which always lasts right up to the point where they need to go to sleep, and then they all want to sleep with a sister, if not in a heap of four. I think most of the not-wanting-to-share-a-room mumbling has more to do with wanting to have their stuff left alone than it does with actually wanting to sleep alone. And heck, I want them to leave my stuff alone too, so I totally get that desire.

But yes, I do try and hide from my kids from time to time. When my energy is higher and it is not the dead of winter I tend to get up before them. It's always a toss up between doing the things I should do (like maybe getting work done early, writing, or getting some exercise in, in peace and quiet) versus doing what I want to do, like read a book without being interrupted on every page, watch a show, or work on a craft project. All of those things sounds really nice and yet are hard to do with kids around.

My hubby and I often run away on Sunday mornings for some coffee or tea somewhere just to have an uninterrupted conversation without the kids. In the past we have tried walking first thing in the morning (and that worked until every morning was below freezing temps), and we do have some time at night now, but running away on the weekend is really nice as well.

But especially when I am under the weather or super stressed out, I like to spend time away from my kids. I don't want to share or take my stress out on them, and when I am not feeling well my patience level is stretched thin.

However, there tends to be a lot of guilt about taking time away from my kids. I am not sure why. I don't feel guilty going on vacation from my business. So why should I feel guilty about taking time away from my kids? That's like a fuller and more demanding job (without yearly evaluations or built in levels of support) than most careers. And most careers have vacation time. So why the guilt? Why not just say, hey I need a few hours off every day and I need a day or two a month off? That shouldn't be so hard, right?

But it is. Mommy guilt runs deep in our society. You are supposed to be there for every game, performance, and extracurricular activity. But you don't want to be. There is something lovely about dropping your kid off and then going and doing something else. This is probably more poignant for me since my kids are at home all the time, because I don't just send them to school and have breaks at my job or just stay home without them. But that also means that my guilt about not wanting to always be there seems like it should be less, because I am there in quantity. Over and over and over again.

Which is probably why I sometimes hide from my kids. Because honestly, most of the time being a parent is pretty boring. And stressful. At any moment you can go from a happy-go-lucky moment to needing to deal with an emergency situation. Let's not even talk about the emotional rollercoaster most kids go through on a daily basis, day in and day out. No wonder we feel like a crazy person half the time.

SELF-CARE FOR GROWN-UPS

There is a lot of stuff in the news and popular media these days about self-care. There was even a trending article just before the holidays that argued that self-care is not about chocolate and luxury and is instead about actually making a budget for your household, etc.

I would like to argue that self-care can be all these things, and that for grown-ups, it often depends on the day.

For me self-care can sometimes be as simple as getting away from my kids. Right now I swear my 4-year-old is clingier to me than she was as a baby, and just having a few minutes when she is not touching or whining at me would be absolutely wonderful!

The occasional breaks I take to go get my hair cut, to go grocery shopping alone, to go on a business retreat, or to take extra training at Girl Scouts can be a lifeline for me.

But equally important is time with friends. Even if my kids are still there and are being their normal interrupting chicken selves, having time with friends is better than staying a hermit in my house. Truly.

Hiding in a hot bath and reading a book is one of my go-to things when I need some extra TLC or am just feeling under the weather. Most of the time I can sneak it in without any of my girls joining me, though occasionally it ends up being a family affair.

When it is not bitterly cold outside, drinking a hot drink with my hubby out on our back deck is lovely. The kids tend to either play in the yard or find that it is slightly too cold for them and go inside. It's great because we get some much-needed vitamin D and a gentle start to the day.

But sometimes self-care is getting that uninterrupted time to actually do something, be it have a conversation with your hubby, do your taxes and set a budget, pay the bills, or actually de-clutter the top of your dresser without having to explain what each item is. Just doing these things is super important.

Sometimes it looks like stealing a few minutes to finish a chapter of my book, or getting in an extra two rows of knitting. Or actually getting to finish my food without someone else insisting on taking some bites or finishing it for me.

These are important things. Dragging my kids on a walk or a hike even though they may talk the whole way does seem to really help our relationships and at least gets us all outside.

Making yummy treats just because the day ends in Y is also a fun thing to do, like spontaneously ending the night at a friend's house.

We schedule regular game nights or afternoons with friends, partially so we can have a chance to play games with people over the age of 15, or at the very least spread the teaching of good sportsmanship around. But also because we have found it's a great way to connect with other families and other adults while still including the kids.

Sometimes self-care looks like moving furniture around to make for a better flow in the house, so that things can work better, or just to change things up so that things flow in a different way.

Sometimes it is getting to garden without extra help.

Sometimes it is their insistence that you have to stop what you are doing Right. Now. And play with them or read them a book.

Sometimes it is not telling them their best friend is coming over until just before they arrive so they don't ask you all day how much longer it is until their friend comes, when they just asked two minutes ago.

Sometimes it is just taking a deep breath and knowing that this too will pass, that this stage will change and that helping small people learn to take care of themselves and discover their own self-care is one of the most demanding jobs we can ever attempt to do.

There is beauty in the attempt and the imperfection. There is beauty in the fact that we all mess up and it will never be perfect, because life isn't perfect and there is so much for our children to learn from the imperfection of our lives and the impermanence of it all.

Like self-care moments that you hope will last at least five minutes and instead get shattered in two. And so you try again as soon as they are distracted again.

WHY DO WE CALL THEM GUILTY PLEASURES?

If it gets us through the goddamn day and helps us have patience around these little beings that depend on us, why should we feel guilty?

Why is it that pleasure equals guilt? Especially when you are a woman. Reading a trashy novel is something you are not supposed to admit to, just like watching *Scandal* and other so-called "trashy TV" shows. Honest to God, if you are able to read every day I don't care if it's "trashy" or not. Some statistics say that only 1 in 4 adults read at all after their formal education is done, so if you're reading, then bravo!

If you are watching trashy movies or television when your kids aren't around, or sneaking in some episodes while hanging out in the bathroom (don't tell me I'm the only one doing that?), that should be fine too!

I truly believe that it is okay to step outside of yourself every now and then, and that doing so can sometimes give you a different perspective when you step back in. It is okay to need to escape. While the meditation gurus might disagree with me, how many of them are raising kids right now? Isn't meditation a form of turning the world off and just focusing on yourself for a few minutes, to quiet your mind and all that stuff? Have you tried doing that day after day when your kids are interrupting you?

Yep, that can quickly turn into feeling like work, whereas reading or watching something trashy does not feel like work. It feels like an escape, and that is a much better break for your brain for a few minutes.

What's perfect is when you can combine doing something with your kids and getting your needs met. Like when the book you are reading aloud to them is actually well-written and exciting (and there are so many other choices than just Harry Potter), and you can discuss it with them between reading sessions.

Occasionally we find a good family-friendly show we can all watch. Lately we have had to resort to YouTube and watching videos of farmers and things like that to find something everyone wants to watch. For some reason, my kids are completely enthralled by watching ration packs being opened and tasted. Not sure where that is coming from.

But there are times when you can't. You need something light and fun when you are traveling; you just do, even if you are the driver. We listen to audiobooks as a family in the car to a certain extent (usually only just one direction) and then I have to put some music on (usually not One Direction – see what I did there?). But I totally miss when we had a working DVD player in the back seat, because then they could watch a DVD and I could listen to an audiobook of my choosing, and that felt really good and made the driving at least more tolerable.

I get super bored super quickly if I am just hanging out in a bathtub without something to do. I prefer to read, as I find listening makes me feel sleepy, but again it feels good to have something like that to do. I also feel that way about packing and cleaning, so having something like that to listen to will actually make me want to get those things done. Well, I'm not sure there is anything that will make me *want* to do them, but I want to have the end result where they are done.

Let's zoom out to the larger picture here for a minute. There is a lot of backlash about women having pleasure. Whether it is sex or other forms of enjoyment, it is always wrapped up in *forbidden* and *guilt*. Hell, even marketing chocolate to us - and let's face it, we would eat chocolate regardless of how it was marketed because, DUH, it's chocolate! - has to be all *guilty pleasure* and *hide it from the kids*, etc. I get the hiding it from the kids part, so it's actually there when you want it, but the rest of the stuff - is it really necessary?

So I say we stop hiding our guilty pleasures and start being proud of them! Did you read a book that is better than *The Hunger Games* or *Fifty Shades of Grey*? I want to know about it so I can read it too! Is there a show you are binge-watching? I want to know that too. It was because of a friend's share on social media that I found *The Marvelous Mrs. Maisel* and that show is hilarious. I need another season right now!

By sharing our pleasures with the world (in safe environments, obviously, as not everyone needs to know our pleasures) we not only take them back, but we are also demonstrating to our kids that pleasure is valuable, that it is a valid emotion just like all the others, and that we can and should enjoy it regularly.

Does my pleasure look like yours? Probably not exactly, but if we are honest about what we do enjoy, not only can the Universe give us more of it, but we can also pave the way for the next generation to not need to put the word "guilty" in front of it.

THE WIND IS BLOWING THROUGH THE TREES

The wind is blowing through the trees
And the sky is gray and full of clouds
It is the first
stormy day on the horizon but not quite
Here yet
Day I have gotten to sit and spend in my new
House,
In the rural life we are creating for ourselves.
Everyone else is still asleep and
The rain is not quite falling.
It will be soon
But not quite yet.
The anticipation of the storm
The anticipation of the cooler
heat
and the humidity
being sucked out of the air
Is still here.
The anticipation of it all getting ready.
The crickets are still chirping,
Which they do all day here.
My curtains are blowing but
My windows are open at the top

Because I am on the second floor.
It feels like it's going to be
the cozy kind of day
To curl up with a book and
a craft project
To listen to an audiobook
Or get out a board game
And play.
Hygge with a warm cup
of tea,
snuggles on the couch
With overly wiggly children.
But right now
Everyone is still asleep.
There is a profound silence
Only interrupted
By the classical music I have
playing in the background
and the occasional deep
breaths I can hear from my
slumbering family.
The breeze blowing through
All these oak trees,
I being the person to find
The oak forest to surround our
property instead of the traditional
Maple trees that Maine is so famous for
Yet oak trees are my favorite
And so it feels like home here
Even though instead of
being cozy in a chair
today
I really need to get back to unpacking
And putting things away,
Finding the missing bookcase shelves
and sorting all the books

And going through the boxes of
errata and miscellaneous and
debris
From our life
And keep what we need
And donate what we don't
And just let it all go.
That's what I really should be doing,
Hanging up our art and photographs
And organizing our tea.
But right now
I am going to enjoy this early morning quiet
With the cloud cover it should last
extra long today
Where the loudest sound is the engine braking of the
trucks
out on the highway.

CRAFTING FOR SANITY

I love to craft. It's not something everyone does or understands, just like from the outside most people think that having four children is a handful. I think the proper term these days is "maker." I like to make things with my hands for the pure joy of making something. Not just for the feel of making, but I usually like the end result as well.

I grew up with makers, at least on the female side of my family. Both of my grandmothers were always doing some kind of handwork, as well as my mother and sometimes my aunts. I had to spend a lot of time in waiting rooms growing up because my brother was at therapy appointments, and in those days before cellphones and tablets and everyone having the internet in their homes, there wasn't as much to do, especially since I didn't enjoy reading until I was 11 or 12.

So I learned to craft. I started with cross-stitch and plastic canvas and eventually learning crocheting, knitting, and sewing, along the way making my first skirt at age 10. This has continued throughout my life, including the four years I worked at a fabric store. I love crafting.

These days I am usually found sewing, (either by hand or with my machine - we currently have four sewing machines in the house not counting the serger), knitting, or crocheting. This remains my happy place and was the first place I had to find again after having kids.

I had to make time to craft again first as I came out of having all my little kids. I am sure I made things in and among having them, but I never really prioritized it. Now I do. There are a couple of things I need to do every day to stay sane. Regardless of being a mother or a wife, these are just basic to my way of seeing, experiencing, and processing the world.

One of those things is reading. The other is making something, or rather working on whatever project currently calls me. Just like books, I usually have more than one underway. I am currently in the middle of knitting two sweaters. One is very simple and straightforward and the other one is complicated, so they both serve different needs and parts of my brain and time.

I also have several quilts and other sewing projects in process. Unfortunately, the power plug for my preferred sewing machine got separated from it during the move and I haven't found it yet, so I haven't been able to take it to the shop to get tuned up and have its tension fixed. This is of course putting *me* under some tension and I will need to fix that soon. Being in a new house, there are a lot of small sewing projects I want to do, like making potholders, curtains, and the like.

I am super lucky that my husband is also a maker. He makes different kind of things. He likes woodworking, brewing beer, and painting tiny metal miniatures, but just like me he needs to do these things to process and experience his world. Which means that we have a respect for each other's work and are able to come to agreements on budget and creating time for both of us to meet these needs. While I don't always understand his craft and he doesn't always understand mine, I respect that it needs to happen and that he needs the time and space for it.

Crafting with kids can be hard. I don't just mean crafting around kids, because we won't talk about how many times my kids have caused me to drop stitches or gotten into what I was working on. Plus my crafts don't tend to be done in a single sitting, so they do have to have a place to exist while they are being worked on, especially the handwork projects.

I mean that creating the space for kids to start crafting can be hard. I love taking my kids to programs where they get to do arts and crafts and I don't have to do any of the set up or clean up. I love watching my kids explore their world through learning new things and playing with materials, without any preconceived notions or thoughts that it has to be done or look a certain way.

That being said, it's hard to have their craft supplies everywhere. It is hard to have to sweep up the glitter, the sequins, and the scraps of paper from all over the house. Slime is currently banned from our house because of cleanup issues. There was a while where I refused to make homemade playdough because of all the places I kept finding it.

I know it is important to share these things with my kids, and I do try. But it is also important for me to have my own stuff and for them to respect it. I am happy to help you learn how to embroider or do that thing, but please, please, stay out of my yarn and fabric.

I mean, unless you really, really want to see Mom lose her shit in an epic way, you will stay out of my craft stuff. That and my books, and you may live to adulthood.

I LIKE MISTY MORNINGS

I like misty mornings. The way the fog is starting to cling in the fields behind our property. The way it is darker in the mornings, so my kids are less interested in waking up early.

I like how puffy our long-haired cat is, getting out in the humidity that clings to everything. I like how bouncy my only really curly-haired child gets in this weather.

I don't care for the boob sweat. For feeling like sweat just clings to me and doesn't go away. I don't care for the fact that I still haven't set up a light in my new office yet. I really do need to get on that soon.

I prefer the mist and fog to burn off by 10 am so my kids will have plenty of time to go outside and play. That it isn't always a rainy day. We need rain, so having it sometimes be a rainy day is good, but a constant string of days soon gets tiring on my ears and my kids' ability to speak nicely to each other.

It is still pretty warm, just misty, and the air is heavy rather than it being cold and miserable or just plain hot. Perfect *cup of tea and a good book or an audiobook and something to knit or sew* weather. Not good hanging the clothes outside weather. Not that we have hung a clothes line yet anyway. Soon. We will get there soon, or do it next spring, one or the other.

This should be a quiet week, as there are are only two events outside the house for library programs. We may go camping with friends overnight on Saturday, providing we can find someone willing to put our ducks to bed and let them out again in the morning. If the weather gets better I might set up some playdates. Or I might not. Having a quiet week at home can feel good too.

I am still working on unpacking and organizing, just not at the feverish pace of before. I'm working on it in chunks rather than trying to get a whole room done in a day. Now it's about maintaining and reminding the kids that they still have to sweep and put away dishes and clothes and all that fun stuff. That bathrooms still need to be cleaned regularly and maybe I will get one of them to run the vacuum later today. It certainly needs it.

I haven't gotten all the laundry picked up and put away in the adult bedroom yet. Why is it that our room always seems to be the last place to get cleaned up? Part of the issue is that my hubby got gifted some clothes a while back and now he has more than he currently needs. He'll need them later, as things wear out, but figuring out what to do with them in the meantime can be difficult. However, I got a lot of it started and picked up yesterday.

I am going easier on myself this week. Not pushing so hard. Taking breaks and time to sit with cats, read my book, or play games on my tablet while listening to an audio book. I need to start moving the plants out of the sunroom and into other parts of the house so they can do their job of cleaning the air.

I need to find my sewing machine cord. I need to plug the printer in so I can print the updated instructions for the sweater I am knitting. I need to be able to occasionally watch a video without all my kids showing up and talking over the instructor.

I need to go on a date with my hubby. I think he is organizing it this time around. Something about seeing a friend of his in a musical – not his usual cup of tea, but if he is offering to take me to a live musical I am there in a dress and a grin. We don't have enough time or money to go to all the plays we have available here in Maine. It's just not possible.

I need a few sleep-in days, a few days to just be. I'm not sure when I am going to get those, as right now I need to write and get some of my work done before my kids wake up, with all their needs. One is already up and lying on my office floor. It is officially only ten minutes after seven, which I know for some families is late and for others, like mine, is early.

SELF-CARE WITH YOUR KIDS

How do you get your kids involved in your own self-care needs? Because let's face it, if you can get them involved then at least their interruptions are a bit more controlled. Also, it counts as quality family time, right?

Over the years I have tried a bunch of different things, some of which we still do and some of which we only pull out occasionally. Family life changes and so do my needs for an oxygen mask and the list of what my kids will put up with.

- Foot baths. It's pretty simple to set up, especially if it's warm enough to do outside. I usually pull out all the big mixing bowls, roasting pans, etc. Fill them with nice warm water, and maybe some essential oils like lavender, or perhaps some rose petals. Some good river rocks to rub your feet on are nice as well. Whatever works best. My girls have always thought this was great fun. Just don't forget the towels to dry your feet off with afterward.

- Hiking or going for a walk. Yes, it can be a pain in the ass to get them all sorted and together, but once we get going, I almost always feel better, and they usually do, too. They can most often be as loud and boisterous as they want, and get all those wiggles and the need to run out. This can be done in almost any weather, as long as you are willing to deal with the mess when you get home. Baths and hot drinks are good once-you-get-home possibilities, as well as packing water and/or snacks for the journey. I usually just take water if it's a neighborhood walk. If it's a hike, then snacks are included for the summit or halfway point.

- Taking a bath. You can give them a bath first and then take one yourself, or let them all pile in with you. This works for showers as well. Depends on your current level of tolerating being touched, but it can be just the way to connect as well. In the summer, going to a local body of water can serve the same function.

- Reading a book. Yes, sometimes it would be nice to read something for yourself, but often I can find a children's book I can stand to read and can read to them for a while.

- Watching a movie. Family movie night, afternoon, or all day because you just need it are also possibilities. We have been known to watch a lot of how-to stuff on YouTube or Craftsy as a group as well and at least that feels educational. Speaking of which, nature, science, and technology documentaries should not be overlooked, as well as cooking shows. Thanks to Netflix and Amazon Prime this can all be done without ads, so it doesn't increase the *I Wants*. Then of course there are lots of good classic British Whodunits, which usually work no matter the age of your children. When we were cooped up in the middle of the summer dealing with chicken pox, everyone got to pick one show to watch and Mom got to pick every second or third show so I wouldn't go mad for the 72 hours I was physically holding my children.

- Naps. Take them together or let them watch TV while you take one yourself. Set an alarm and tell them they can't come and bug you before the alarm or timer goes off. We often do lie-downs when life gets overwhelming. You can read, color, or listen to an audiobook in your bed with your head on the pillow. Heads on the pillow and little to no talking are requirements. It gives everyone a break, even if you don't lie down yourself.

- Nail polish. We have amassed a small collection of Piggy Paint nail polish which is pretty much non-toxic and best of all doesn't smell. While it won't lead to perfect painting, letting my kids paint my toes and/or fingernails is something they find grand and I can just sit and be for a few minutes. They often get together and do each others' nails as well. I find pieces of cardboard for them to put hands and feet on, which keeps the mess to a minimum.

- Going to the park. I am not a hover mom or one that necessarily gets involved at the park much. Beyond pushing you on the swing it's really up to you to go and have fun. I need to stretch, read my book, or listen to an audiobook while we are out here in nature absorbing the sun.

- Going for a car ride. This can be a nightmare or it can be relaxing, but no matter how loud your kids are, if they are still in boosters or car seats, at least you know they are safe. Put on a family-friendly audiobook or some great music and off you go. Usually they come back calmer at the end of it. We find peppermints and gum essential to ward off car sickness, but really this can be a go-to family activity when you've had enough of your house.

I hope you find some of these things helpful. This isn't the only way I get self-care, and if it was I am not sure it would always work, but these are great ways to get some extra!

WHAT HAPPENS WHEN YOU LOSE YOUR MOJO?

It is going to happen. It turns out that sleep deprivation is more deadly than food deprivation (and let's face it, most of us are making bad food choices when we are sleep-deprived, but we are still eating!) and you can't be a parent without some sleep deprivation. It just comes with the territory.

I have been extra tired lately, and by and large I am not getting that much interrupted sleep anymore. We no longer have a child sleeping with us and my hubby and I really don't argue over the covers too much. I have been working on getting the light levels down again (thanks to children and their need for nightlights in a new house) so you would think my sleep would be improving.

I am getting regular daily sunlight, exercising in the morning, not having any caffeine after noon, and drinking lots of water. So I keep expecting my sleepiness to abate. But so far that's not happening.

I am working to make more space in my schedule to rest, including taking the occasional nap. I am also making sure that I am doing things that feed my soul every day, like knitting, crocheting, sewing and reading or listening to audiobooks.

I am working on keeping the dust down and the clutter at bay, which is hard since we are still in that beginning stage of a new house, where we want to unpack but we really don't know how the flow in the house is going to work yet, so we unpack and then end up needing to move things around later, again and again, as we figure things out.

But I am tired. I have even been going to bed early the past few nights and it has not made getting out of bed in the morning any easier, although I am getting more than eight hours of sleep.

My hormones are regular, as near as I can tell, so I suspect that I am simply in the process of paying back all the energy I used earlier in the year.

But it is making weekends difficult. There are things we want and need to do on the weekends, and frankly I just want to be left alone. I am not feeling a huge need to be super social. I have more out and about time, now that all the fall activities are taking place.

I thought originally it was just my cycle, that I was PMSing and that was all that was going on. But now that I am on the opposite side of my cycle and still feeling this need to draw in, I think maybe it is just fall.

Anyway, here we are. My kids don't necessarily feel the same way, being kids. I am not even sure if my hubby feels the same way, as he finds all the building and working on the homestead to be relaxing, and I don't always find it to be that way. I am glad to do the sawing and lifting and moving because, hey, it's exercise I don't have to think about, but sometimes I am just too tired to care.

I can't even argue that I am under the weather, because while yesterday was cold, it was sunny. I think the constant change in the weather, being cold one day and then warm a day or two later, is not helping things either. I am never fond of transition and I prefer the seasons once they have made up their minds. I like to know whether I need to wear my thermals today or not, without having to check my phone.

So I am acknowledging the change in season, both the outer changes of the weather and the change of season in my life that also seems to be going on. My youngest is almost five, which means that babyhood is coming to a very definite end. My eldest is 12 with the body of a 15-year-old, so we are very definitely moving into the teenage years.

I will be 40 in less than 18 months, and society tells us that is a big deal. I am not sure if it is or not. I didn't think 25 or 30 was that big of a deal at the time. But I also do not want to go back to those ages either.

I am supposed to be envisioning what I want in my personal, family, and professional life in the next five years, and it's hard. So many amazing things happened in last five years. But I know having a target to aim at is better than just wandering around like a lost person. Time ticks on regardless.

THE SILENCE OF THE MORNING

The silence of the morning
Before anyone gets up
When the day feels fresh and new
and your eyes are groggy still
The fuzziness of your brain
Is creeping round the corners
Of your mind
But the alarm has gone off
And as a mother
Of children
You know
If you don't get up now
and enjoy
The silence of the morning
It might never
EVER
Happen
Again.

MOM SUPPORT IS LIKE LEGOS - YOU DON'T WANT TO STEP ON IT IN THE MIDDLE OF THE NIGHT!

As mums, we need support. We need friends to complain to, share cute stories with, and connect with. We need partners to take over sometimes when we have had enough of what our child has done.

There are so many other ways we can ask for and receive support, but we have been taught not to. The pinnacle of our society is to DIY everything, especially our lives – and, well, sometimes that just doesn't work.

Like the stack of legos that is probably somewhere in your house, when it is built into something it doesn't annoy you or bug you and hopefully it keeps your children entertained for a while. But when the pieces are scattered and you end up stepping on them in the middle of the night, that just really hurts, and I don't know about you, but swear words are imminent from my mouth.

Not having support is like that lego piece in the wrong place. Your emotions just start coming out sideways. But also like legos, you can build your support brick by brick and over time and you can remove support that you no longer need or is no longer serving you and replace it with pieces that work for you.

So often we feel like we can't ask for support. And then when we do (often in whiny, bitchy voices, let's be honest) we then nitpick what we receive. No one wants to help a control freak, and does it really matter if your kids got fed pizza for dinner and stayed up a half an hour later than normal if you got a night away from them?

For some kids and families that would matter, but I have found that for me it is key not just being able to ask for support, but also being able to gracefully receive support once I have asked for it. I know when I go away for 3 days for my business retreat that my hubby will probably let my kids watch way more TV than I normally do. But that's okay. It's only for three days, and he's taking time off from work rather than me having to find child care for those three days.

When I ask for help getting the kids to do their chores, it might not look as perfect as I would like. Asking anyone else to clean means that it isn't always done the way I would do it, but sometimes it is actually done better.

I know it can be hard. I have the tendency to say *yes* to things before thinking them through and then being annoyed later that I volunteered to do that thing. I have learned that certain situations bring this out in me and I have put in different checks and balances so that I have time between the request and my answer. It's not 100%, but it is getting better.

Where can you get support? Can you ask if your kid can carpool around an activity? Can you trade playdates with a friend so you get time alone and you get other kids playing with your kids for awhile, and your friend gets time off too? Can you let Grandma take your kids and have them stay long enough that she deals with the sugar crash?

Just like building with legos, you get to pick how your house looks. You can decide what the most important foundational pieces of support are for you. I've shared some of mine here, like reading, crafting, hiking, and just walking outside when my kids are too much. What are yours? What would you like to invite into your life? Don't get stuck on the money, because often if you want it badly enough you will find a way to get it anyway, whether it costs money or not.

You need to build your own support structure and not just have pieces scattered on the floor to step on.

One of Those Days

Parenting Sucks

Parenting sucks. It really does. All the cleaning up of gross messes and picking up after small creatures that seem to strew stuff behind them like ever-increasing tails.

All the sickness, snotty noses, and coughs. I swear, with four kids it seems like someone is under the weather pretty much all the time.

And don't get me started about the amount of food they eat, and don't eat but demand to have anyway. And the mess and dishes that requires.

Their cute little clothes that then get quickly ruined by accidents, get lost under furniture, or they just outgrow in the blink of an eye.

The amount of baths and showers you have to give, cajole, and monitor. It doesn't get easier as they get older. because it just gets to the point where they refuse to get clean, even more so than when they were refusing because they didn't want to go to sleep.

The stories you have to read that might have been fun the first time around but by the time you get to the 100th-and-something you can read it in your sleep – and you do.

The number of times they have woken you up from a sound sleep or just as you were drifting off and now you can't get back to sleep.

The number of times they got between you and your sex life. By either interrupting, sapping all your energy, or literally sleeping between you and your partner.

And then all the stuff you have to help them be responsible for. That pet they begged and begged for, that in a perfect world they love and look after, but you still have to buy the food for and who occasionally gets sick and just ends the world.

All the sports, school, scouts, birthday parties, and stuff that you never had to budget for or spend time organizing or thinking about before.

All the craft projects that they love to do and really enjoy, but then what do you do with all the shit they made afterward? Because you can't keep it all or you would literally drown. You can mail some of it away to relatives (although that takes a whole other level of organizational skills), but let's not talk about the environmental impact of all that art hitting the trash. It's not like you can really compost macaroni art.

If you are a type-A personality that likes to have a schedule and a routine, then having kids is always going to try your patience as they inevitably interrupt, get sick, or otherwise change your plans (because, you know, they didn't behave the way you wanted them to, so your consequence was to keep them home instead of going to that social event).

And I am sure you can think of a bunch of other un-fun things I haven't even mentioned here.

So why do we do it? I mean other than the fact that none of us really had a complete idea of what we were getting into when we decided to have children. All that excitement over a line on a test didn't really prepare us for who we were getting on the other side. So besides the fact that we have made this commitment to these small creatures, what keeps us showing up each day?

Is it those rare smiles that just light up their little faces? Is it the fact that they can make us laugh like no one else can (even though sometimes we have to struggle not to, because it really isn't appropriate to laugh just then)?

Is it those freely given hugs and kisses and the way they are almost always happy to see us?

Is it those cute faces? I am not kidding, I think kids are cute as a survival mechanism. It seriously convinces us to keep them alive longer.

Or is that someone might have done these things for us and we have a vague memory of it?

Or maybe for the exhaustion we feel at the end of the day?

Or maybe because we know that someday we will get to rest and the monsters (ahem, kids) we are protecting and parenting will have monsters of their own.

NO-GOOD-VERY-BAD-DAYS

Some days you wake up and you might as well go back to bed. You just know it is going to be one of those *Alexander-terrible-horrible-no-good-very-bad-days* kind of day. But you're a grown up. You probably have a list of things that you need to do today – maybe an important meeting, maybe just a house that looks like an tornado walked through it, or maybe you are providing child care for someone else's kid.

The no-good-very-bad-days don't show up when you have space in your schedule. They don't show up when you feel like everything in your world is going great. They don't show up when you have nowhere you need to be, or no one you are responsible for.

No-good-very-bad-days show up when you are super busy. When there is so much that needs to be done, or you have had some very big changes in your life, that to add the shit frosting on top of the shit cake, here it is. A day that you just know isn't going to be a good day.

Maybe you feel like you are starting to get sick. Maybe you *are* sick. Maybe your kids wake you up with them being sick. All over you. Or they are running fevers and put their hot bodies up against yours.

You've got two choices. You can get up and get this no-good-very-bad-day started, or you can try and get some extra sleep. Hit the snooze alarm a few times, or just ignore it altogether. I have done both, so absolutely no judgment here, regardless of your choice.

Throughout your no-good-very-bad-day you have choices. You can pretend that you have an assistant (or maybe you are lucky enough to actually have one) and cancel everything that is not super critical for you to do today.

You can call in sick. Play hooky. Decide to binge-watch TV with your kids. (Secret from a summer of chicken pox: let each child pick one show and rotate, including yourself in the rotation so you can watch something that you have picked every now and then too.) At the very least, you can prioritize what absolutely has to happen today and punt everything else.

Oh and give up on the meals. Pass them off to someone else, get someone else to cook, or decide that it's going to be takeout tonight. Or cereal and milk. Or popcorn. If you absolutely can't get out of cooking supper then make it breakfast-for-dinner. It's usually super easy-going.

You can also decide to stack your day and try and get through those most important things first. Get that load of laundry started, get dinner in the crock pot. Don't stay in bed because your children are still asleep and you can get your work done early, or at least get started on it.

Try to laugh. On a no-good-very-bad-day you might not want to wear your best clothes because you will be spilling stuff on they. Make sure your helmet is on and you've buckled your seat belt. Take some extra moments to breathe. Pass off as much as you can to someone else.

See if you can have a mommy playdate so someone else is helping watch your kids and you can compare your no-good-very-bad-day with another mom. Not in the competition sense, but in the *we all have these happen from time to time* sense. I have a friend who hangs out at the children's section of her local library when she, as she puts it, "needs adult supervision." It can be helpful to just put your kids in a new safe environment with extra adults who may be helping to keep an eye on them.

It can also be helpful to just cancel everything and stay in bed. It's not something we can always do, but it can help.

I often try and get the priorities done first so that I can later take a nap, an extended siesta, or just curl up on the couch and read to my girls for a while on no-good-very-bad-days.

Remember to take your vitamins! They can't hurt and will probably help. Go slow on the caffeine as getting super buzzed is not going to help and may contribute to the no-good-very-bad-day. Drink water. My go-to solution for everything that ails you: go have a glass of water, and then tell me how you feel. Of course, you may end up wearing it.

That's okay. It's only water. So it will be wet, and either cold or hot, but it shouldn't destroy too much. I wouldn't have any alcohol until you have reached the finish line of the day - see the above caffeine advice.

Maybe sit down and actually read about Alexander's day, and see who had it worse. Your kids will probably enjoy listening to the classic. Hopefully you didn't have a dentist appointment, and maybe you really could move to Australia.

Of course, in my experience with Australian airports, I am not convinced you would actually have a better day there, but you never know. It might be better in Australia.

Tomorrow most certainly should be better, especially if you can go to bed early tonight. Because no-good-very-bad-days are exhausting.

SOME DAYS I JUST FEEL SICK

Some days I just feel sick. It's hard to get going or to be going at all, to rise out of bed and put one foot in front of the other. That part has little to do with being a mom. I mean, I would get sick before I was a mom, before I was married, before I had an obligation to anyone other than myself. But it seems so much harder to just turn the world off and not feel well once you have kids, once you have those obligations, because, well, something always needs to be done.

I don't think my hubby really suffers from the man flu. Not really, not the way it is portrayed on the media. He's not completely helpless and if he needs to do something even while he is sick he will. He's not going to die if someone isn't there to take care of him.

That being said, it is rare that we are both sick at the same time. Really rare. I feel like because he can just take the time off from work, he can succumb to the misery of being sick and then he can get past it. But I just have to keep going. Sure, I can maybe clear my schedule and take a nap, but I still have to find a way to feed the kids, and make sure the dishes are getting washed and the cat is fed, etc. I can't just lie in bed for days and have someone else check in on me. I remember last year I happened to get sick on a weekend with a fever and I was able to spend most of the day in bed, reading a book on my tablet and sleeping, and it was glorious to just be sick. But it was one day out of the whole year, and I am pretty sure I got dragged down to eat dinner with the family, which felt like too much at the time, it really did.

I feel like because of this I never get time to just be sick, and therefore I end up not feeling 100% for more days out of the year than if I just took a couple to be truly sick. That really just sucks. It is so tiring. I don't like not being 100% and having to fight through my day tooth and nail instead of just sleeping all day in bed and possibly feeling better the next morning. I mean, it's not guaranteed that I would feel better, but I probably won't feel 100% the next day because I am just trying to claw through this one, or at least that is how it feels. That is what it feels like going through it.

It's this uphill battle of being sick. Especially when the kids aren't. Especially if it's just me and him and he can take the time off and I just have to keep going, keep going and make sure all the balls are in the air, or at least most of them, and I am just so tired. I just want it all to end so that I can get some real sleep without anyone else in the bed, because spending four nights next to someone with a fever is not real sleep. Not really. It's more like sleeping with a thrashing toddler.

NO ENERGY

Some days we have no energy. As mothers there is just nothing left. We are stretched thin and there is nothing but the thinnest piece of skin between us and the world. If you touch it, if you blow on it, if you make it vibrate with your noise we just might get torn, be swept over the edge, and have that be the end of us.

We most certainly will lose our shit. It will be gone, lost, and what might erupt out of us is Goddess-Kali-like-volcanic-energy. We might swear, shout, scream and throw a tantrum that would put our two-year-old in the corner in a ball. We might just completely and utterly lose our shit.

No one wants to see that. We don't want to admit that it even ever happens (but it does, you know it does when we are pushed too far). So instead we ingest large quantities of caffeine, chocolate, sugar, or alcohol.

We find a way to binge-watch TV or to pick a fight with our spouse, because we are going to blow and if we don't take immediate action, the mess we are about to make will not be pretty. Not a fucking pretty sight.

This is not something our kids deserve to see, or be on the receiving end of. But I guarantee that most of us parents can't make it through getting our kids to adulthood without at least one major scream-fest. Some of us just try and keep it down to once a month or quarterly, but I guarantee that it happens.

Does it have to be this way? Can we look back and find ways to keep ourselves from being so stretched thin that the slightest breeze tips us over the edge? Is there any way to prevent this colossal blow up from occurring? Can we keep it from happening?

Well, your road is different than mine. But here are some of the ingredients that I have found that add to the recipe of blowing up for me:

- Not getting enough sleep.

- Not getting enough help.

- The house looking like a total shit hole and no one but me gives a damn.

- Too many social events and not enough time at home.

- Driving for days.

- Not enough time to read a piece of fiction.

- No time to work on creating something with my hands.

- Life stress, like moving.

- Not eating good food.

- Not enough sleep – oh, did I mention that one already?

These for me are some of the key ingredients that make a volcanic explosion. Notice that baking soda and vinegar are not required. However, not using them to clean things can be an ingredient.

Can I control some of these? Sure. I can do my best to go to bed at a decent hour (though whether or not I get woken up is not necessarily something I can control).

I can allow my kids to only sign up for one extracurricular activity at a time. It won't kill them to choose just one. I have four kids, and it might kill me if they do more than one.

I can say no to social events, or more importantly, keep one weekend day a week where we stay home, period. I don't care how amazing your social event is, it's not as amazing as my blow up next week because I didn't get any time off.

I can hire a housekeeper. I haven't done it yet, but you better believe it is on my bucket list, because my kids are not reliable cleaners....

I can make sure that I always have access to a good piece of fiction and that I can at least sneak away to read for five minutes a day.

I can have craft projects strewn across the house so I am never far from one I can make.

I can speak to my hubby about my needs when they are not being met and find creative ways to get time off, like a long bath, a nap, or just a sleep-in day. Or maybe he could just make the next couple of meals for me.

These things and more can happen and when they do the explosions get further apart. I am more often able to see they are coming and find a way to head them off, or explode away from my kids so they don't have to be a part of it.

Will they ever truly go away? I don't think so, because I am human. Part of being human is losing your shit from time to time. Some of the most valuable lessons in life come from the shit-losing.

Sometimes the only way to make space for something new is to lose something first, and yes, sometimes that truly is our shit.

Sometimes those explosions turn out to be massive crying events rather than scream fests. Just sayin'.

SOME DAYS I JUST WISH THEY'D GO AWAY

Some days I wish my kids would just go away. Don't get me wrong - I love them and can't imagine life without them. But honestly, some days I wish they would just go away.

I suppose if I sent them to school I might not feel that way, but then the pressure of work would take its place, because if your kids are all school age, there is no reason for you to not be working outside the home, right?

I don't think it's because I run a business and do occasionally need to think straight without my interrupting chickens, well, interrupting. I remember wishing they would go away and I could get a break sometimes even when I was the one working outside the home, or was the stay-at-home parent without a business.

Some days they are just too much. They talk too much, demand too much, need to be corrected for abhorrent behavior too much. I can understand why so many of us lean on technology to babysit them, because we just want a few minutes of peace.

For me it gets worse when I am tired or sick. My tolerance for the touching and the need to follow the long-winded imaginary story just goes out the window. It's difficult. It's not their fault that I feel this way, just as it's really not mine. My poor hubby gets to take over more of the cooking and other household duties because by the time we reach the end of the day, I am done and just want to curl up into a ball and be left alone, which doesn't necessarily get his needs met either.

It is not a lot of fun. I do my best not to have too many of these days. Usually one or two per moon cycle I can plan for and just work around. But this week I think I have hit a wall. I think it's partially because we have had a crazy spring, with looking at houses, then buying one, and all the ups and downs that brought, and then moving in and wanting to unpack for a party and now I just want to absorb what little summer seems to be left. I think maybe I burned the candle at both ends for a while and now my body is just demanding rest.

I was grateful that my eldest didn't want to do the library program today because she feels like she is coming down with a cold and didn't want to spread it to anyone else. Not only was that good forethought for an almost 12-year-old, but it gave me the excuse to get work done this morning so that I can then just sit and read this afternoon. I have a good excuse for that. I have about 300 pages of a book to read between now and Thursday morning, and it's already Tuesday.

Yesterday was a hard day even though I ended up getting a nap. I was hoping today would be better, but last night I had lots of disturbing dreams and got woken up several times by the black cat trying to convince the gray cat to play with her. The gray cat decided to have none of it and hissed up a storm. Not exactly how I was planning on waking up this morning.

However, I do have a late-in-the-day beach date scheduled for tomorrow and the other mom doesn't care if one of my kids might have a cold. My girls have been missing beach time so hopefully this will help. It should be a shady spot, so that should help as well. I am thinking about not sharing it until tomorrow so I don't get the infinite *when do we get to leave* questions.

I am just so tired. I want to curl up on our new-to-us couch or easy chair and be left alone for a day. I think that would help me feel so much better. Maybe not. But it is all I am itching for. This week is less busy, which is good, but it also means everything can catch up with me. And that doesn't get the laundry or the dishes done.

It's not like the girls do much housework without me constantly reminding them to do it, which takes energy in and of itself. But I feel like if I don't and I just do it all myself they are not learning valuable lessons and I am going to get really resentful.

That's my idea anyway, and I'm sticking to it.

WAKING UP SICK

When the whole house wakes up sick, it really does feel like everyone should just go back to bed.

Almost like if we were on an airplane and someone else came and brought everyone warm drinks from time to time. And crackers. Crackers are usually good when you are sick.

I am thinking an international plane, so everyone has their own TV screen to listen to music or play games or watch TV on, from a curated selection of movies and TV shows so the kids can't just watch anything, but if they want to watch *Frozen* over and over again they can. And I can be in my own bed watching what I want to watch and getting hot drinks delivered regularly.

And someone else is in charge of cooking the meals, doing the laundry, and cleaning the bathroom.

Yep, that would be perfect.

Of course none, of that happens. If everyone in the house is sick, then you know there is a case of the man–flu going on. My hubby is often good at tag-teaming if he is not really sick, but if he's really sick, forget it, he is down for the count.

I don't know what is worse, fevers and aching bodies, or the stomach flu with vomiting and diarrhea.

I always think whichever is not going on is the worst.

But then I change my mind the next time we get something.

I think head colds are hard because you are not 100% well, but you totally feel like you should be, and you make yourself go to work, and take your kids all the places and everything, but really all you want to do is curl up on the couch and veg, or in my case it's usually take a nap.

Naps are wonderful. If I can't sleep they are a great excuse to get caught up on my reading. Which I never get caught up on, because I love to read, but anyway. I could go on and on about the type of book you need to read when you are sick because they are able to actually take you out of your misery, but I won't digress that far.

None of my kids are at the point where they will read when they are sick. So that just leaves other forms of entertainment. Thank the Gods that audiobooks were invented and live in lovely clouds named Audible. That means they can listen to the Penderwicks, Land of Stories, or All Of A Kind Family ad infinitum and I don't have to read it out loud to them. I just need to be in another room or they need headphones.

Seriously.

Today they all want to take baths, but my eldest, at 11, does not want to take a bath with anyone else. I totally understand, I feel that way too, and try to be graceful when they all have to pile in anyway. But when I am sick, forget about it.

No extra touching, please.

Actually, how about no touching at all?

Because I know where you hands have been and I really don't need anyone else's snot to deal with. Mine is annoying enough. Trust me.

I am just so glad I am past the point of a snotty baby who needs to nurse. Because there is something about snot on my breasts that grosses me out on a level that no amount of vomit and poop has to this point.

I say that while knocking on wood, because you know, I am not about to tempt Fate and her mistresses.

But seriously, I am not a human-size handkerchief or napkin. You can keep your snot to yourself.

I have plenty of my own over here.

LOW-GRADE FEVERS

Low-grade fevers - kids get them all the time, from the time they are babies and teething until, I don't know, the early teens? My eldest is only 12 and she still gets them every now and then.

As adults, by the time we get a low-grade fever and we are no longer surrounded by doting parents, we often have to muscle through whatever we have on our schedule anyway. We still have obligations we have to meet, homes we have to take care of, pets, children, and partners to feed.

Sometimes we can call it all in and call it a day. Sometimes we can tell our invisible assistant to cancel all of our appointments and reschedule. Sometimes we can feel the fever coming and clear our schedule ahead of time. Those are the good times.

Often, though, we can't see a way around what we have planned to do. Or if we do decide to call out for pizza for dinner, we feel like a failure afterward (because let's face it, pizza is not going to help us heal from this stupid fever) or we feel like we are being judged.

Because the moment we don't feel well, we start to feel like everyone is looking at us (even though, with the exception of our children, probably no one is looking at us). It is frustrating. But it is real and it happens and we get under the weather.

Then what? How often do we keep going, keep pushing, trying to find ways to still get everything done with time that is slipping away too fast because everything is taking longer because we just can't think straight? We just can't wrap our heads around what is going on and *would everyone please just shut up and turn all that noise off?*

Maybe we ignored the first signs. Maybe we barreled through them and now it's near the end of the day and we still have to drive home and we are oh, so very tired.

Maybe people are counting on us. Maybe we were actually feeling good a few minutes ago. Maybe that last crying session by our kids was what threw us over the edge. Maybe that comment on social media that was meant to be nice just stings so much.

So what can you do? Now you are here and you don't feel well but you usually can't drop all of your balls yet. What do you do?

I try to stop and take a deep breath and look at what absolutely has to happen. I need to be in a safe mind space to drive everyone home. Does that mean I need to get a drink, or pee, or buy a coffee, or get some food? Do I need to listen to uplifting music or an audiobook or silence on this drive home?

Can I ask hubby to make dinner, or can I pull something out of the freezer? Is it really a good time to bring home something easy for dinner (minus the pizza as that usually just makes me feel sicker; your mileage may vary)? Does dinner just need to be cold cereal and milk for the kids and maybe a hot cocoa for me? Can I go to bed early or take a nap for a few minutes between obligations today?

How can my partner support me? Let's double up on some vitamins, that can't make this situation any worse, right? Can I take a bath after the kids go to bed, or while they watch TV? Is there a friend who can take my kids for a while?

There are almost always ways to clear your plate at least a little. Can you sleep in for a few extra minutes tomorrow morning? Going to bed early is almost always an option. Can you get someone else to go to that meeting? Can you lean on another parent to carpool to that after-school activity? Can you get some other kids to come over and play with your kids? I swear that usually takes less energy than my having to entertain my own kids.

Most importantly, what can you put in place for the next time this happens? Because there will be a next time. You will get under the weather again. What can you put in place (including actually getting that assistant who can clear your schedule), so that next time it will be easier and you can just let it go and take care of yourself?

I guarantee you will feel better faster if you just surrender. And maybe eat some bone broth.

PLAY WITH ME

The cry of every small and not–so–small child everywhere: "will someone please play with me?" It has become more of an issue lately as my eldest, at age 12, is less interested in playing imaginary games as each day goes by. My 4- and 6-year-old don't always get along anymore, and since they have grown up with two older sisters to interact with them, they tend not to just play with each other.

But this weekend they are going to have to. My older girls are going overnight camping for two nights and my hubby and I will be home with just the younger two. We have things we need to do, so it can't just be a *play with me all day* kind of weekend.

There are parents who can sit down and immerse themselves in the imaginary games of their children and parents like me who really can't anymore. I can sing silly songs, tell stories, and read lots of picture books, but please, please, please don't ask me to play an imaginary game. I'd rather deal with sore losers and sore winners while playing a tabletop game than have to play an imaginary one. I guess my brain needs to have some kind of framework, some kind of rules. Or maybe I have simply been sleep-deprived for so long that I am not sure what my brain does like anymore.

Maybe it's the limitlessness of it all. Like I could go on wild-tangent games for say, half an hour, but I can't do it all day or no one is going to have anything to eat. It just isn't going to work.

I remember reading *Fierce Kingdom*, which is about the three hours in which a mom and her four-year-old son are hiding at the local zoo because someone is shooting people. She will do anything to keep her son quiet. I totally get that. While I have not been in that kind of life or death situation with my kids (thank goodness), I have certainly been on public transportation or an airplane and really wanted my kids to be well-behaved and quiet. Waiting rooms and checkout lines come to mind. I have been so tired from a nursling that I have let my other kids watch TV way longer than I should have just so I could take a nap. It feels like negotiating with terrorists sometimes.

Maybe this is like meditating and something I just fail at. I have tried meditation for years, off and on. Pretty much anytime Deepak Chopra and Oprah hold another free 21-day meditation I sign up. I think the longest I have made it is about eight days in a row. I usually end up falling asleep.

I know the research. I know meditation is supposed to be good for my brain and I really should learn how to do it. I prefer walking in the woods or knitting, personally. I find my brain stops its constant spinning when I do those things. I have yet to find that while chanting *Om*.

And I am done with judging myself about it. I haven't found a form of meditation that works for me. Hell, I am still working on a regular morning walking practice, but I figure every day it happens is better than any day it doesn't, and some days sleep is actually more important.

It is the small everyday steps that matter rather than the big juicy moments. Those matter too, but our life is made in the small steps. Things like deciding to get up in the morning, making sure everyone is fed, making sure to take some time for yourself, even if that means binge-watching TV, or in my case, starting a new craft project before I have finished the last one.

These are the things we do. This weekend is going to be interesting because my hubby and I have some computer projects we want to get done, and yet our younger two will just have each other to play with. I wonder if the neighbor kids will come and play. I am not sure who they like to play with the most, so not having the older kids might matter.

Only time will tell.

ALL THIS *AND* RUNNING A HOUSEHOLD?

FAMILY CHORES

There was recently a discussion on Facebook about chores, inspired by a video where a grown-ass woman was cleaning the room of a near-adult child. It sparked the question: how much do you clean up your kids' space?

I have vacillated about this. Because on the one hand, I totally think it should be my kids' responsibility to put their damn stuff away. On the other hand, if they never see what a neat and tidy room actually looks like, will they get a chance to try the peace that comes from everything being in its place and having clear surfaces that aren't covered in clutter?

I did not grow up in one of those households. I grew up in a household full of books (at one point we had over one thousand) and all the wall space had furniture and just about every flat surface had stuff on it that rapidly became clutter.

I have been fighting this for years now, having lived outside my family of origin's house for a while. I did not marry a neat freak, which I knew as soon as I saw his bedroom with his dirty and clean laundry both on the floor – and I am still not sure to this day how he could tell the difference.

The funny thing is that anytime I have worked in an office, I have been neat. I keep hotel rooms and hostels and even tents as neat as possible. I honestly think that if I ever live alone for any length of time my house will be neat and well-displayed without clutter everywhere, outside of a small stack of books by the bed and partially-finished craft projects by the sewing machine and where I hang out at the end of the day.

But I have never in fact experienced that. I went from my house to living with my husband, and moving and having things in storage and not having enough time to really unpack...

Now I have four kids and have lived in three different houses with them in the past 7 years. So it never feels like we are done with the packing and unpacking life. We are currently looking for land and another house so that we can get out of renting and again that will cause upheaval.

But still, I am drawn to neat houses. I don't mean showrooms without any life, I just mean kitchen containers that are actually clean and toys that are put away and fridges that don't have food stains on the bottom.

And yes, I do clean. Sometimes I feel like all I do is clean, and it is not something I enjoy. It is not a driving force. But I know I feel better when my bed is made, even though I have to do it every day. I know that I work better in an uncluttered environment. But I will be totally candid here and say that I swear the moment I sweep my office floor one of my kids troops in and leaves a dozen *troll droppings* all over it.

It's not fair. Why do I have to always clean up after them? Why do I have to lose my patience at them? Why can't they actually start their chosen chores before I scream at them at the end of the day because I have reminded them at least half a dozen times?

I have tried to be a good example. I have tried to show them that I do chores every day. I clean up after myself, and I put things away. I take time every weekend to clean up a clutter-y part of the house and I try to create systems that work for how we actually live and use the house. Because we homeschool, we have people here more than not, so I swear that makes for a messier home. Maybe it doesn't, but it sure feels that way.

I have not gotten to the part where I just want to give up this battle. I do want to put a sign up that says *chores in progress – teaching children* so I don't get judged about the fact that my 11-year-old still hasn't washed the dishes, because she needs to learn the consequences of that several times over, apparently. I am seriously getting rid of most of their clothes and soon, because they have way too many and they just make a mess.

Will I ever live in a clean, organized home? Is that even possible? Can I learn the behaviors and habits? Probably. Will I make enough money to hire a cleaner? Probably.

But at the end of the day I know that I would prefer to knit or read a book over cleaning. If it weren't for audiobooks I would get even less done. It is just not my favorite thing and probably never will be.

GOVERNMENT AGENCIES WHEN YOU HAVE KIDS

Trying to talk to government agencies when you have kids has to be a special kind of torture.

I mean, on the one hand, if you are a stay-at-home parent it should conceivably be easier for you to actually make a call during the work day because you're not, like, actually working.

But that is not taking into consideration that magical thing that happens the moment you go to pick up the phone to either answer or to make an important phone call.

Your kids show up out of nowhere. And they need you. Right. Now. Because it's an Em.Er.Gen.Cy even though you had checked on them and made sure they were fed, watered, toileted, and entertained before you even contemplated making said phone call.

Everything was good, everyone was fine, it was all good.

So you take a deep breath (because who knows how long you are going to be stuck on hold, it could be forever) and dial the number.

Maybe you are safe for a while. Maybe you do in fact get stuck on hold for a while. Perhaps the kids stay engrossed in that television show you would never normally let them watch, but that you are letting them get away with just this once because this call is important.

But then it happens. You actually connect to a human being on the other end of the line and you start exchanging important information.

Maybe you are just a weensy bit stressed out about this whole thing and that is what causes your children to show up out of nowhere. Maybe it's just your tone as you put on your extra polite, somewhat pleading voice. Or that funny laugh you have when you are trying to explain a mistake and get the buy-in of the person on the other end.

I am not actually sure what it is, I just know it happens. The whiny, whinging child shows up. Usually with their voices turned all the way up as far as it is possible for them to go.

Usually they are extremely obnoxious and ignore your signals that you are in fact on the phone trying to conduct a polite adult conversation. Even when they are 11 years old and warned ahead of time that you are going to be on the phone, they still come stomping into the room you have squirreled yourself into, all bent out of shape because they need an answer to their problem immediately.

It might be the baby of the house who decides to start pulling on you and yanking on you and otherwise needing you right now.

Maybe someone decides they need to poop right now, or worse still, need you to wipe said bottom.

You try to excuse yourself to the adult on the other end of the phone and explain that you'll be just a moment, or that it's vacation week or something, while you are willing to bribe your child with anything if they will just leave you alone for a few minutes!

It's enough to drive a parent insane.

Which is why if it is at all possible I would rather email, online chat, or write you a snail-mail letter than to actually have to pick up the phone and deal with a real live person on the other end of the line.

Because if I have to do that, my kids are going to show up at their worst. And if you are not a native English speaker who can speak off-script we are already going to have issues.

Not to mention that no one really wants to hear the screaming kid in the background, do they?

I sure don't.

There should be a special playground or something where you can bring your kids and they are going to be so absorbed in what they can play with that they don't notice that you need to pick up the phone and deal with some important issue.

That would be awesome.

Maybe I can find some mother friends who also need to make phone calls and we can trade off? I wonder if that would work? There should be a code word or secret handshake or something.

MOVING

I have done a lot of moving in my life. By the time I was 14 I had lived in five states and eight houses. As an adult, the moving slowed down for a bit. But since we moved to Maine on Labor Day weekend of 2010, we have lived in three different rentals.

Now we have a house under contract for another move. Hopefully one of the last. We have been in our current rental for almost four years, so most of my kids do not remember moving at all. Last time we switched rentals, I literally moved the house myself, with our SUV and multiple trips back and forth and back and forth while my mom stayed with my kiddos at the new house and my hubby helped on the weekends.

It was so tiring. I got a lot of audiobooks listened to, but it was exhausting. I would literally stay at the new place long enough to nurse my not quite yearling and then I would make another trip, loading and unloading on my own. I think my hubby would help me do one trip after dinner each day, but I really can't remember.

This time around we have a little more warning (closing is six weeks away, so it's closer to eight weeks until we have to be completely out of this house). I have an 11-year-old who can help with the loading and unloading. The 9-year-old, possibly, the 6- and 4-year-olds, not so much.

I am hoping to get a bunch of friends and/or teenage boys to help us move the bulk of it on a weekend, and then just have smaller trips to do after that. I am dreaming of a line of people bringing everything down from the attic and most of the upstairs and just ferrying things out the door and into a truck and then out to the new place.

The new house has a full basement, so my dream is that all the boxes can go down there. The furniture can get put in the rooms they are probably going to be in (you always end up moving things around about a year to 18 months after you have lived someplace, once you really understand how you are using the space), and then the boxes could be brought up one at a time and unpacked.

There is a ton of stairs and lots of lifting in my near future. It's a good thing I have been getting at least 1.5 miles of walking in every day. I don't think I have to worry about much weight-lifting in the near future.

The house we are moving into has one extra bedroom and way more closets. We have four closets in our current rental, and we are moving into a house with 12. That's a huge difference. I am so excited about our pantry and closet off the dining room (which will most likely become the tabletop game closet because eventually the dining room table is going to be a game table too), and the two linen closets upstairs. I mean, I will actually have a place to store spare sheets for each bed. Imagine!

We are also moving onto two acres which will mean the ducks will have more space, the hop garden can expand (oh the happiness of my husband knows no bounds at the moment), as well as other more permanent gardens becoming a reality. I can plant asparagus and rhubarb and roses now!

The full basement means better storage for out-of-season stuff as well as the laundry room being down stairs. There is also space for my husband to do all his beer brewing and have his workshop down there. Eventually we will probably build a two-car garage on the property, as that is really the only thing it is missing.

This next eight weeks are going to be stressful. It is so hard to not be super excited and yet terrified that things might fall through at the last minute, because until we get to closing and get handed the keys (and then change the locks) it's hard to believe it is actually real. So many emotions.

So many logistics. There are six of us, one cat, and 21 ducks to move. Lots of emotions. Lots of stuff, some of which I am hoping not to move. Lots of trash to go through. So much sorting. Some of which will happen now, and some of which will happen over months while we get used to the new space.

I will be getting dedicated office space, and my biz will get to pay rent – what fun! But also what a lovely thing to have that be part of the way my biz can contribute to our family. So many other things hinge on having closing done, like getting a new cell phone plan and new phones, and getting my sewing machine fixed so we can sew proper curtains.

We will be moving just in time to enjoy the glory of summers here in Maine. Girl Scouts will mainly be over with until the fall, so there will be less driving, many hours spent at the local watering hole, and lots of organizing, unpacking, etc.

This will probably be the move that my kids remember, at least the older two. I hope they don't just remember the chaos and confusion and making new friends. I hope they also remember how happy we are after the move is done, how much more space they have, and how great it will be to paint the walls, add shelves and do whatever we want, because it will finally be our home.

Now to just pass inspections....

UNPACKING

Kids get just as excited about unpacking as we grown ups do. Which means completely mixed feelings, at times joyful to have things out of their boxes and instead up on their walls and shelves, and at other times really not wanting to look at one more box ever again. *What do you mean I still have to unpack it?*

We get to have all the feels, which includes the frustration of having the unpacking seem to take much longer than we would like it to. For me, this hasn't been one of those moves where I can just spend all day, every day, unpacking until I get it all done. Because life still needs to go on and I took my time off for the actual moving from one house to the other. At this point we all need to start falling into a routine again, which means I need to get my writing and work done in the morning while I still have energy and it is still quiet and cool around here, and so unpacking happens later.

Inevitably, it doesn't seem like I have gotten enough done. For some reason that I really can't wrap my head around, we seem to be short a bookcase in the number of books I still have in boxes versus the three shelves I have to still fill. Since the clips to attach the shelves to this bookcase have gone for a walk, it makes things even more interesting. We have a friend holding another bookcase for us, ostensibly for the girls' picture books, which will help, but it would also be nice if that two dozen or so boxes that are usually super easy to unpack and get out of our way, were actually out of our way.

Then there is the building of things. We normally have our flat screen TV up on our wall, so it stays safe – and also because who needs it taking up furniture? We haven't taken the time to install it up on the wall yet, partially because we haven't located the stud finder, and also because the time we would have to install it (it takes both of us) is the same time we want to spend actually using it.

Then there are the racks and pieces of furniture we took apart and now have to figure out where all the pieces are. It is usually not the legs as much as it is the bolts, pegs, and clips. For instance, I have my round table in two pieces and it takes about five minutes to put together, but I don't know where the bolts that secure the two pieces are.

That kind of stuff. We spent part of Sunday in the kitchen building a couple of racks to hold dishes and veggies. It doesn't look like we did much, because things are still cluttered and on the floor, but we did actually create some pretty important storage to be able to start to put things away.

My Mom is coming in a couple of weeks and my goal is to get the main living areas done by that point. Then while she is here and able to entertain my children, I can redo a closet each day and get those set up well.

But right now things are just getting put into closets to get them out of the way while we continue to unpack and organize.

At least the laundry monster is starting to come under control. But I also need to set up an area in the basement for the out of season, out of size clothes, and of course that hasn't happened yet. We did spend some time in the basement over the weekend when it was really hot and that was helpful. It's allowing us to bring the rest of the stuff from the yard into the basement, but still, that part of the house isn't something you see all the time.

I had a friend come to help yesterday and we were able to organize and unbury two rooms in the two hours she was able to help me. I am hoping to convince some more friends to come over to visit and help us figure out where to hang our photographs and art because I know that will help it feel like home on an even deeper level.

I am aware that it is going to be a work in progress for a while. There is wall paper throughout most of the house and we are going to want to work on taking it down and painting most of the rooms over time.

It also just takes a while to figure out the flow of things and how things really work and then move things around accordingly.

There are pieces of furniture we do not yet own and that need to be acquired to make the cozy reading and talking nooks we still want to make. There is stuff in the yard that still needs to be set up for future gardens, hops, and of course duck land.

In and amongst all that, it is still summer and we need to find the local swimming holes and places to hang out in the shade, attend library summer reading program activities, and do some actual reading. Eventually my sewing machine will get fixed (still looking for the power cord) and then there are lots of little projects that need to get made for the new house as well, like fresh potholders, new curtains, etc.

Everyone has always told me that when you own your own house the honey-do list is never-ending and there is always something that needs to be done. But I think the part that a lot of people have been missing, that seems super important to how my hubby and I feel, is that this feels like a labor of love. Getting to choose and adjust things because it is our house. Making a list of the maintenance as well as the upgrades we want to do and knowing that we are taking care of our shelter just feels different than having to wait until landlords fix - or don't fix - things.

Or at least that is how it feels to me.

NEW KITTY SNUGGLES

My husband and I have had many cats in our lifetimes. Growing up, my family got our first cat when I was 11, and by the time I brought my husband home for the first time, we had our fourth cat and currently had three living with us.

My hubby and I decided we wanted to start a family and tried for a month and didn't get pregnant. We both worked in retail at the time and Christmas was coming, so we decided, the heck with this, let's put it off until next fall and in the meantime let's get some kittens. We went with a breeder because I am allergic to cats and we had heard about these Siberian Forest Cats that might be hypoallergenic.

After spending several hours at the breeder's house around her nine cats and kittens and not getting sick later, we picked out two boys to adopt once they were old enough to come home with us. We picked up Shere Khan and Mishka the day after New Year's and found out five days later that I was pregnant with our first child.

Timing, right?

Fast forward 11 years and many houses later. We have since lost both of our dear boys, as well as Tchaikovsky the Maine Coon cat that asked to come home with me from the animal shelter that was hosting him at our local pet food store. He was three when we got him and fit right in with Mishka, who was desperately missing his brother. Unfortunately, two falls ago we lost both Mishka and Tchai within about six months. It was really hard.

Last Thanksgiving we got gifted a friend's cat. Our friend discovered that she was super allergic to cats and Charlotte, her cat, likes to drool, so was even more allergenic than a normal cat. We took Charlotte home with us on Thanksgiving to our empty-of-cat house. She was coming from a house of seven kids, a dog, a bird, and a lizard, and thought our quiet house of only four girls was a lovely place. She still often shows up when we are having playdates with other kids, as if to say, "the house is finally as full as it should be."

Charlotte is a sweet short-haired cat, and she's indoor-outdoor. What's great about that is that she only uses the litter box in the dead of winter and the rest of the year goes outside. I ignored her a lot when she first moved in, so of course she decided that I am her favorite person, as the logic of cats goes.

Last week I was at the library, where the kids reading program is helping to support one of the local animal shelters. They have put up displays of some of the cats that need to be adopted, and as I was walking by I was compelled to read one about this father and son that needed to be adopted together. Since neither cat was a kitten (13 and 1 year old respectively) I thought they might be perfect, since Charlotte is around eight. I called the shelter and asked some questions, and planned to go down and see them the next day after talking things over with hubby.

Of course by the time we got there they had been adopted (which was wonderful as they had been there for over six months) and I was left with four children who were hoping to bring two cats home. I asked if they had any Maine Coons as they don't make me sneeze, and they pointed out some kittens, which frankly was not what I was going for. I have four children under the age of 12. I know my limits.

But we did go into two cat rooms and ended up meeting several lovely cats. The one that wanted to come home with us was an all-black long-haired female who is two years old. She liked kids, and let all four of my kids pet her and interact with her. She was unsure of dogs and only likes certain other cats. After seeing all the cats and coming back to this one several times, we inquired and then adopted her and brought her home.

I wasn't able to do the whole *keeping the cats in separate rooms for several days* thing you are supposed to do. My bad, I know. So far Charlotte isn't in love with our new cat, but she is slowly coming around. The new cat thinks Charlotte would make a great buddy and doesn't understand Charlotte's reluctance. But we haven't even had the new cat for a week yet and we know it takes a while – how many times have we added to the duck flock?

Then there was the issue of the name. The new cat came with the name Lulu, which I felt wasn't distinguished enough for her. I mean, look at our former cat names: Mishka, Shere Khan, Tchaikovsky, and Charlotte. I grew up with cats named Isaac, Orion, Ashes, and Roary. My hubby, on the other hand, grew up with more cutesy cat names of Dusty, Casper, Rocky, and Mercedes. So his suggestions revolved around Fuzz Butt.

We finally decided to name her after Nymphadora Tonks from Harry Potter. The cutesy faction can call her Tonks and I can call her Nymphadora or Nymph.

HOUSE PARTY

You never know, here in Maine, when you invite a bunch of people to a house party, who will show up. You can usually count on the people who say they are not coming to uphold that and actually not show. They are usually good like that.

Of course, some of the people who say they are coming will come. Never all of them, though. In all my years of hosting and going to parties here in Maine, not everyone shows up who says they are going to.

Then there are always the maybes. It's a toss up whether any of them will show. But if you are hosting a party with any kind of thank you gift, or you're providing all the food, you can guarantee that most of the maybes will show up, so you had better count them in.

This open house party was really a toss-up. I got a couple of new maybes with less than 24 hours to go, and some more no's. One of my daughter's dear friends (and her family members, who are becoming new dear friends to our family) had a family member in and out of the ER that week, so I wasn't counting on them coming.

There were a couple of people who were supposed to drop by in the beginning for an hour or two and they never showed.

But in the end, the magic worked out just fine. We had one of our dear close families show with one of their kids. We had two families where we know the parents but are still getting to know some of the kids.

It was a really nice new circle in some ways. One of my friends asked how I knew two of the newer families that came, and it was fun to say that one of them was a Daisy in the Girl Scout troop I run and that the other two of the girls are in my 9-year-old's troop. It was fun to get to see this mainly new group of people who didn't know each other talk about their towns and the state of the world without getting into politics or arguments, but rather in friendly discussions about how can we change the world for the better.

Meanwhile, the kids discovered the hill that comes just off of our front door (this being Maine, it's not the door that everyone goes in and out of when they arrive) and were taking all manner of wheeled contrivances down the hill. They were working very hard not to crash into the grown ups, the electric duck fence, or each other. This provoked my loud announcement that sledding parties will be hosted at our house this winter. Please bring your kids and some sleds and I'll provide the hot cocoa and the hill.

There was major use of the plastic play house we'd moved from Florida eight years ago and to every house we've lived in here. It got moved and rearranged several times during the gathering.

There were several pool noodle fights that ended in one pool noodle being broken, but no injuries among the kids, Considering we had kids from ages 4 through about 13 attending, I consider that a great success.

We had an almost 8-week-old with us who I got to walk and bounce to sleep several times. She is a super easy-going baby and seemed to enjoy the party.

I hadn't figured out how to have a table outside for food, so after our first two groups of guests arrived, we ended up moving all the chairs down under the shade of the big oak trees that will soon be hosting a swing. We brought the chips and salsa down there, and in the end we had a picnic on the grass of everything but dessert. The kids got their sugar rush in running up and down to the house to get another cupcake or rice crispy treat.

There was the normal gathering of all four of the guys surrounding the barbeque and talking while cooking the hamburgers and hot dogs. There was plenty of co-parenting going on, with adults taking turns helping the kids get food and drink, and generally having a great time.

Just before the last groups left, when it started to get dark and we all moved inside, everyone helped bring up the dishes from the yard. Yesterday when we went to pick up, there were very few things out of place that needed to be put away, and only a few rolls to chuck at the delighted ducks.

I think having the watermelon rinds thrown over the fence to the ducks was some of the best entertainment for our guests, as some of them have never seen how ducks love to clean out watermelon rinds.

It was a good party. Everyone seemed to have a good time. Kids were whining about not wanting to go home at the end of it, and my kids slept in the next day.

It felt like a good way to introduce the new home to our energy and our friends. I am looking forward to many more play dates, game nights, and gatherings of friends.

ACTS OF KINDNESS

We so often focus on acts of kindness for people outside of our family, especially for strangers and people we don't know. I think it goes back to that concept of "a man's home is his castle," and therefore he can act like a tyrannical king at home and treat the people he lives with poorly.

Yet when you start a relationship with someone who you want to live with for a long time, you don't start it with the concept that you are going to end up being a bitch to that person. The sparks of falling in love are not about being mean to each other or about petty insults, like no one emptying the trash can because you are each waiting for the other person to do it.

That is not where it starts. That is not how you feel about that newborn baby you hold in your arms for the first time (before the sleepless nights start). You want to protect, shelter, and love them, and most of all be kind.

But being a parent isn't always kind. You have to let your kids figure things out for themselves. You have to allow them to pay the consequences of their actions or inactions, within reason. You have to help them process their emotions, while often times being told you have to ignore your own. It can really suck at times.

We are moving and had a huge clean up and packing day last Saturday. We pay to have our garbage picked up every Tuesday (rather than needing to haul everything to the dump on our own) and our current rental does not have any kind of outdoor shed or garage.

My girls had three or four bags full of trash in their bedroom alone, not to mention other places around the house, so we have quite a bit of trash. Last night my hubby helped my eldest, who has trash duty, to take the non-food-based trash out so she wouldn't have to do it all before 9 am, when she has just woken up for the day. This morning, however, we discovered that (most likely) the local skunk got into four or five of the bags and, well, you can imagine the mess.

I should also mention that it rained all night and is still raining. My hubby was all about suggesting I wake the two older girls up early so they could clean up the mess. But I decided to grab some gloves and pants (because I had only just gotten up myself) and clean it up for them. Because it's not their fault that the local critters got into it, or that we haven't bought more trash cans to put the extra trash in (because this is unusual for us and we do not normally have this much trash).

I picked up the split-open bags and did my best to clean up what was scattered. Being wet, there is only so much I can do until it dries and I can sweep it into a pile again. However, I did not take all the bags down to the street. I left the ones in the trash can for my big girl to do. I just took care of the split messy ones.

Yes, I could have left them all for the girls to deal with. But since there were factors outside their control, it didn't feel like the right thing to do. I am not looking for praise or even thanks. As a Mum, I know that cleaning up disgusting messes is just part of the job. This is one of the main reasons I do not have a dog, because four kids and a cat are enough to deal with. I think if I had to clean up dog poop I really would lose my shit. I think it's helpful to know my limits.

There is going to be more trash that gets broken into over the next couple of weeks, I am sure. We close in eight days and will start moving our stuff immediately, but we will be keeping our trash service at our rental until we are done, rather than figuring out how it all works in the new town immediately. Since our current service is the same price regardless of the number of bags, we are just going to keep filling it until the end of the month.

There may also be extra food-smelling trash in the next little bit, as we rely a bit more on snack and convenience food while we are switching kitchens and moving the pantry around. Having quick ways to get more fuel at both houses is going to be required for a while. The drive between houses is about 30 minutes, so quick food is going to be essential.

I am sure this morning is not going to be the last time this month I will have to clean up trash, and definitely not the last time in my life. I am not sure how we will choose to secure the trash at the new place, as the shed has yet to be built and the garage is a couple of years down the road most likely.

I am sure there will be times when my daughters need to pitch in and help with cleaning up strewn-around trash as well. I don't think it was necessary that they needed to do it today. Not with their higher need for more sleep so they can be civil human beings to the best of their abilities while their whole world is changing.

Yep, I think that's enough for them to deal with today. I think this small act of kindness will help things run smoother. I don't have to think about it anymore or remember to get them up in a few minutes so they have extra time to take care of the trash. I can just move on with my day and hope that more of it is sweet-smelling.

IT'S ALL ABOUT SHOWING UP

Parenting is like writing this book.

It's about showing up.

Consistently, reliably, on time.

Whether I feel like it or not, whether my hair is having a good day or not.

Showing up, and putting out content, showing up and loving my daughters, however they need that to look today.

Every single time.

Without the ability to see if what I am doing is really working, if it is failing, if anyone at all is listening.

But still, I show up.

On the good days, on the bad days, and most importantly on the mediocre days. Those always seem the hardest.

Here I am. Are you here? Is there anyone out there?

What does being part of the Mommy Rebellion mean to you?

What does showing up, no matter what, look like in your life?

LIVE AND LEARN

TEACHING PATIENCE

Teaching patience in a digital age where everything can come in nanoseconds is such an interesting parental concept.

I grew up in that teeny-tiny gap generation from 1977 to 1983. Before the Millennials, but after Generation X. My childhood was analog, but my teenage and college years were digital. So I kind of bridge and understand both, and yet it is so important to me to teach my kids patience.

I remember what it was like to be a small kid and be stuck in that idea that it *needs* to happen *right now*. But when I was growing up, things didn't happen right now. You had to wait one week to the next week for a TV show - you couldn't binge-watch a whole season in a day. My kids totally want to do that when a new season comes on Netflix or Amazon Prime, and I am like "No, no, save some for tomorrow, don't binge-watch it all in one day!"

It was so funny when the *Grand Tour* came out on Amazon Prime. You know, the car show. We usually watch *Top Gear* when everyone is sick, because it's this innocuous, slightly funny show, doesn't harm anyone, has no swearing, and it isn't cooking. Because watching a cooking show when your tummy is upset is a *really* bad idea. Anyway, when the *Grand Tour* came out and Amazon would only release one episode a week, my kids were like "OMG, we have to wait a whole *week* for a new episode?"

These are lessons in patience.

Patience. I think this is one of the reasons why it is so important to get kids involved in gardening, besides the fact that digging in dirt is a natural antidepressant. Plants don't just grow overnight. I mean, even with my husband's hops, which can literally grow six inches in a day, it's still a good way to learn patience.

My almost-11-year-old has ducks, and we recently got more ducks because we needed more females. We got a duckling. My 11-year-old kept being worried about the duckling, and we kept saying it's only for a few weeks, in a few more weeks it is going to be a duck. She's had it for six weeks, and it is now much more of a duck than a duckling.

These lessons in patience.

I recently broke my ankle hiking, and it's been a little more than three weeks since I broke it. I wasn't doing anything crazy – this is a hiking trail I have been up at least a dozen times before and I am sure I will go up a dozen times again. But I slipped on some rocks and broke my ankle. Ever since I broke my ankle, every single night, my 9-year-old comes to say goodnight to me, because I am sleeping downstairs in a chair to elevate my ankle, and she says "I hope you feel better in the morning. I hope your ankle is better in the morning."

And I get it. I get that she wants everything to come back to normal. It is never going to come back to the normal that it was before, because that is just not how life works. Everything changes. I tried to explain this to her, but I think it is one of those things that you just have to experience.

But the other thing I want to say is that it's not like pain is linear. I mean, we would like to think it is, that every day we are healing we are going to get just a little bit better. But healing is like grief. It comes in waves. It's cyclic or spiral or cylindrical. You are going to have bad days, days when it hurts more or you can't do it, where you've got to push more, or days when the grief just overwhelms you. It's going to happen.

It becomes part of you, part of your soul, just like grief does. It can be five or ten years down the road and that pain can come up again, because it is part of who you are. You will be reminded of it, if nothing else.

Teaching kids patience is like teaching kids about money these days, because money doesn't exist, it's all invisible.

Teaching kids patience means trying to explain to my 5-year-old and my 9-year-old that their 11-year-old sister is just going through her uglies, and that this is just a stage and she will get better. Right now she is just being a bit of an ugly duckling, but it won't always be about her. Again, an example of learning about patience.

We really do need to teach our children about patience, because as Simon Sendik says about the Millennials generation that I am slightly too old to be in, they were given a shitty hand, a bad set of playing cards, and they don't know how to deal with patience. Because you can order something on Amazon and it arrives the next day, in some places within a couple of hours. So they don't understand patience.

Teaching patience. I think it should be on every parent's curriculum.

How do you teach your kids patience?

MAJOR LIFE EVENTS

How do you prepare your kids for major life events? You know, the ones where you know a little bit ahead of time that they are coming, but maybe not with any certainty. Like when you are trying to find a new place to live, be it a rental situation or a buying a house. How do you have them be a part of that process but at the same time deal with their emotions while dealing with your own? It can often be too much to deal with. Because it is a roller coaster of getting your hopes up and then preparing yourself for disappointment or having things fall apart or actually having things go through and then figuring out the logistics.

My mind is built for logistics. When I found out that in less than three weeks we were going to get expedited passports and travel to New Zealand with all four of our girls for two weeks to attend a family wedding and see a relative before they passed away, my mind went into overdrive.

Like the time we moved about 20 miles away from where we had been renting, and I literally moved everything we owned over the course of two weeks, one SUV load at a time, while my mother watched the girls and I nursed my not quite yearling between each load. Then I had to go back and clean the place we had been renting and that seemed to take forever as just one person. Eventually it was me and my husband, both being so tired that we didn't know when to stop or when things were clean enough (which in our defense is hard to determine in a 150-year-old house where dust falls from the ceiling every time you walk upstairs).

Or the time we moved from Florida to Maine with just our two little ones. Emptying storage took longer than we expected so we had to get up super early the next day to get out of town with the huge moving truck before the traffic in the city got bad.

How do you prepare kids (much less yourself) for this? And how much of it depends on the age of the kid? I mean, if they are under 2 you can probably talk about it around them and they really won't pay much attention. When they are older than that, though, it can get difficult. The older they get the harder it is to A) hide from them what is happening and B) them being able to deal with it well. Because of course they want to talk about it constantly so they can figure out how they feel about it and what their roles are, and you can easily end up making promises that you will either forget about or are impossible to keep when the time actually comes because no matter what we can never actually predict what the experience will be like until we have in fact started experiencing it.

I suppose that if you have kids in school it might be a little easier to have these conversations if you ever have time with your partner and they are not around. That not being my experience, I am not sure how likely that ends up being. It turns out that for my hubby and I, email or messenger can be super helpful ways of communicating some of it. But in the end we often do just need some time to chat things through.

We have a babysitter now that our eldest is 11, but after a couple of months of babysitting she has become a very reluctant babysitter. That has caused problems, because sometimes we really do just need to go sit in a cafe for an hour and hash things out. That can't happen at home with the interrupting chickens and the fact that the walls are thin and we don't want them to hear everything we are talking about.

I really don't want them constantly in front of the TV just because we need to have an adult conversation. Because what is that teaching them, besides the fact that the more TV they watch the less it will work when you need them to watch TV because you need them to leave you alone, for real this time, it's super important? Yeah, that doesn't work if they watch a lot of TV. I speak from experience on that one.

So what do you do? At what point do you clue them into what is going on? Do you wait until all the paperwork is signed? Does it come out in the heat of the moment because you have gotten stressed out? Do you let them see photos on the internet of places you are looking at? How do you look after them as a good parent and yet still handle these life-changing events?

How do you handle getting them ready for an airplane trip that is going to be a 12-hour flight when they have never gotten on an airplane before?

And where does all of your self-care fit into this? Where exactly? Now more than ever is when you have to put that fucking oxygen mask on first, because you are going to need it just to get through the next few days, weeks, months. You really are.

WHY I HIKE

I broke my ankle in August 2017 while hiking up my favorite local hill - or maybe it's a mountain. I mean, it's called Mt. Battie, but that doesn't actually make it a mountain, does it? I digress.

Anyway, it was about the sixth time I was hiking that particular trail with my family. This time we even had a neighbor girl along with us. We were looking forward to getting to the top and picking wild blueberries before coming back down. Hiking has become a weekend tradition for us. Every single weekend.

It was morning and the ground was damp and I managed to misstep while climbing up the trail on some rocks and when I landed I heard my ankle pop. Having broken the other ankle back when I was 19, I was aware of what it felt like and what that particular feeling is. Bone pain is unlike any other pain I have experienced, including the four natural births of my daughters.

We were able to help me limp off the trail and over to the road, before getting in the van and then later going to the emergency room. My hiking boots were a blessing, as was my husband's quick thinking to dump cold water all over my shoe and ankle to help numb it while we got off the trail. I am thankful to have not needed rescue from the rangers.

It wasn't a bad break as breaks go. It was all stable, so no surgery and only 3 weeks completely off of it. Because we had an international visitor and had already booked and paid for our trip to Cape Breton, Canada, we still did that 10 days later even though I was in cast and crutches the whole time.

The hardest part of the whole experience was having to not move, to sit still, to not be able to hike up that hill again.

Because you see, about two years previous we had discovered something life-saving. Our then 9-year-old daughter who was facing all the emotional and hormonal upheaval of preteen life was better when we went hiking. She would often be out front and blasting away and we had to remind her to not get too far ahead (though she does know how to read trail signs and this is a very well marked trail). She was easier to live with for about a week after hiking.

So it became the family tradition to go hiking every weekend. Because it just makes life so much easier. Even though last summer was the first summer we by and large were not physically hauling the youngest two up or down any portion of that hill. Our amazing 4-year-old decided to not be like her slightly older sister and most weekends just goes up and down and only gets tired just before the end of the trail.

We hike because it makes us all happier. We are outside, we are in the woods, we are going up a familiar yet new-every-time trail, and I usually end up with a different daughter bringing up the rear each time we do it. My hubby is usually out front with the leaders and I bring up the rear as the girls are not allowed to be behind us.

We see lots of other people and dogs on the trail. There are folks of all age ranges, though usually not as many families with kids. But our kids love it, so it has just become the culture in our family.

We go hiking once a weekend when there isn't slippery snow and ice on the ground. Maybe we will finally get snow shoes for everyone next year and do it even when there is snow and ice on the ground, but right now, we are avoiding that.

It has been a hard fall and winter for me, healing from this broken bone. I started walking again before the holidays and my body really needs it. But instead of getting up early in the morning and going then (mainly because it has been so frigging cold this winter I would have to be careful not to get frostbite) I have been going in the afternoon with the girls. Does it go as quickly as if I were doing it by myself? No. Do I get the silence I might find when I go by myself (or with my hubby, which we were doing for a while before it got cold)? No. But are they better for it? You betcha.

They are so much better for it. Even on the days when someone is complaining the whole way, and they are arguing as to the route around the neighborhood, they are happier. They sleep better. And they are happier at the end of the day.

So once I finish writing this I am going to go put on my shoes and get them ready to go for another walk. Because this is why we hike. To keep our mental health good. And to move our muscles, and just get along better as a family.

TEACHING READING

Why do we think that learning to read is an easy process? I mean, for some kids it probably is. It wasn't for me, though, so I can't speak from personal experience.

I have four daughters, ages 11, 9, 6 and 4. Right now we are having daily reading practice of at least 30 minutes a day, every day this summer for the older two. My 9-year-old will remind me and eagerly looks forward to doing her reading practice, even though she is still below grade level if she went to a conventional school.

With my eldest it is like pulling teeth to get her to read, and she will tell you that she can't. Which isn't true. She actually can read more than she thinks she can. It's just that she struggles to find things she wants to read that are at her level that are not too boring. Because you know, no one writes early readers for 11-year-olds. You are supposed to be able to read by now.

I struggled with reading. The schools I went to were focused on whole word recognition and I need phonetics. It was hard. I remember how my brain remapped itself when the click happened, and I am trying as patiently as I possibly can to hold the space for that click to happen for my girls. Hence the showing up for an hour of my time every day (and let's face it, it is more like an hour and half because of getting people ready and getting other siblings busy with something else rather than distracting the reader) to hold space for them to read. To work with them to read.

The days where I fail to convince their siblings to find something else to do are the days when they struggle more. It is hard to learn to read in a noisy chaotic environment, and sometimes I still have to leave the room to read because that environment is too noisy for me.

My girls do love stories. I read aloud to them most every day and certainly there are periods where I feel like that is all I do. We have made our way though most of the Harry Potter books this year, as well as a bunch of other middle-grade books. We are a family that loves audiobooks. They are great to listen to while doing the boring parts of life, like riding in the car. My husband uses audiobooks to keep his commute from getting boring.

My girls have grown up with and have access to audiobooks, so there is a love of stories there. They are picky and sophisticated, though developmentally appropriate, in what they want to listen to. All the research says that even teenagers who have been reading for years should continue to listen to audiobooks because it helps make their vocabulary bigger.

So I know that my love of reading, that came late, just around the age that my eldest is now, when the click and brain remap finally happened, can still happen. But I still worry.

There is a lot of external pressure when your kid isn't up to grade level on something, and I suspect it is worse if you homeschool, because everyone seems to think your kids need to be ahead on everything but social skills. Or they are quietly judging you. That's what it feels like.

But part of the reason we homeschool, which is the same reason we chose to have our babies outside of the hospital and without any inducing (even when my 6-year-old was 12 days past her due date) is that it's not about us picking a time. It is about providing them an environment in which they can grow at their own rate, speed, and direction.

So thanks to library reading programs we are committing to, and showing up for regular reading practice this summer, I feel like after 25 hours of reading practice, my older two are going to be further along on the reading-independently spectrum.

My six-year-old is also participating. She is learning to read in such a different way than the other two. She often just needs to be shown a word once or twice and then she knows it. It's amazing, really. Running my finger under the words I am reading aloud seems to be helping her learn to read.

My four-year-old is just happy to sit and absorb everyone reading to her at this point. She often asks me to "do the finger thing," where I run my finger under the words as I read them. But she still isn't at the point where she can write her own name yet. Not that I am worried. She will get there when she is ready and wants to start signing her artwork. In the meantime, her sisters are happy to help her.

I will keep showing up for reading practice. One of these days the click is going to happen, and the brains will be remapped and they will start seeing and reading all the words everywhere. Then I will have to be more careful about writing in front of them, as they will be able to read what I am texting over my shoulder.

But I am ready for those types of challenges, and for even bigger stacks of books getting checked out of the library.

I am ready when they are. In the meantime, I am here. Ready to help and to listen.

THE THANKFUL TREE

Teaching kids gratitude is not, in my experience, an easy and graceful task. At least not for my girlies.

But I know that by training our minds to look for gratitude, to look for the good things in life, we can, in fact, train our minds to keep looking for them. For me and my husband, this is something that is important to teach the girls.

Back in November 2014, the girls and I made a gratitude tree as part of getting ready for the holiday season and Thanksgiving. The girls helped me color in the tree and then they each helped write what was on each of the leaves, and we added to it as the month went on.

For the ages of my girls, this was perfect for their attention span, their need to do everything with their hands, and to have lots of color and texture.

We didn't do it this year, though, partially because I didn't think of it, and also because we have a new piece of furniture on that wall. But we do have a daily practice around gratitude.

Every night as we all sit down for our evening meal, each person says something they are grateful for. Preferably something from that day, if it is time specific, so this time of year you can't simply say that it is one day closer to Christmas, you have to also say something else.

Your piece of gratitude can be small or big – it's all good. Just the other day my youngest actually said she was grateful for one of her sisters, which is a big first for her, and considering how she has been treating them lately, really good to hear.

It is a nice ritual to set the tone of the meal, calm everyone down, take turns listening (because we can't hear if we all go at once), and let everyone have a chance to say something, which in a family of six can be a small miracle in itself at times.

PREPARING TO LEAVE

I have been what some would call lucky enough to have a valid excuse to leave my family for two to three days at least three times a year. For me it is easy. I have a business coach who holds a retreat two or three times a year and it is integral to my business that I attend (I get a lot of my clients through these retreats).

When I first started going, my youngest was smaller, and I actually drove the almost two hours away in the morning and then drove back at night and then did it all over again the next day. I have only ever had to do that once.

Since then I have been able to grab a spot on someone's floor, or these days, share a hotel room, and just be gone for the whole length of time. I still haven't managed to leave the night before so that I am already there and just need to get to the location in the morning instead of doing that two-hour drive. But I am okay with still needing to work on that.

I am getting ready to leave in the morning. I will be gone for two nights and three days. My hubby is taking time off from work to be home with the kids and he is actually really looking forward to being at home with them. Maybe they will do some packing? He is considering taking them on a hike.

I probably won't ever hear everything they do while I am gone. I am okay with that. I have done this enough to know that everyone will be fine. And these days I think it is really good for their relationships to get time together as the five of them without me. I really do.

This summer, though, I am going to be gone even more often. Next weekend I am gone two nights and three days on a Girl Scout camping trip with my 9-year-old. I am not directly in charge, I just get to help follow the programing, and it should be good. Then two weekends later I am again gone for two nights as I

afternoon and my hubby won't even be home yet. The eldest will have to babysit for an hour or two until her Dad comes home.

But I know we will all get through it.

I know that everyone is going to survive.

I know that in a lot of ways we will come back stronger. Relationships will be built deeper among my girls and their Dad. I will have had a much-needed to break to just spend time on me and getting my needs met while growing my business, and making deeper connections with my tribe of women.

I know that I do not have much work planned today and I will probably end up taking them to the park. I know that I have Sunday and Monday off next week so I can just spend time with them and catch up on sleep, as travel always makes me tired.

I know it will be fine. It will be great, even. I am so lucky to have these regular periods of time when I get to step out of my normal life and assess what is working and what isn't and make adjustments. I think we all need that from time to time.

THE GIFTS OF HEALING

I broke my ankle for the second time. Different ankle than the last time, 17 years ago, but I still broke it. Just like before, it came out of nowhere.

The first time I broke my ankle, I was 19 years old and taking my first real vacation from my first real corporate world job. I was at a pumpkin festival with family, swinging out on a rope swing and falling into a pit of packing foam. I was doing it with an over-6-foot-tall guy and he wasn't hitting bottom. But of course, on the last time I swung out, instead of swinging and landing on my back, I managed to get a leg tucked under me and the only metaphor I can use to describe it was that it felt like someone had stepped on my ankle and compressed it, like when you step on an aluminum can.

That was a huge break, breaking both my tibia and fibula and needing surgery and a long recovery. I still have a plate with seven screws on the outside of that ankle and a big long screw on the other side, and scars to show for it. But I did eventually recover.

There were gifts. I read the first Harry Potter book in 24 hours and then proceeded to read the next two (all that were currently published at the time). I had the opportunity to "wake up" and realize that I did not want to stay working in the corporate world anymore and that I really wanted to go be a camp counselor or park ranger and have an adventurous life. I left my job about six months after healing, got a job at my old Girl Scout camp, and then went to France with my Dad who was attending a conference, which in a long way around led to my visiting New Zealand and getting engaged.

So this August, when I was hiking a local trail that my family and I have hiked many, many times before (including at least a half-dozen times this year) while also with one of the neighbor kids, I was completely taken by surprise when I slipped on some wet rocks and fell, having first one ankle tuck under me and then hearing a loud pop from the other ankle. I pretty much knew instantly that I broke it. But I still had to get down off the trail. Hiking boots saved the day.

This fracture has been much different from the first, in part because it is a stable fracture. The bone has stayed in alignment and so it has simply been a matter of providing support while my body works on healing the bone. Did you know you can walk around on a healing bone? My first broken ankle required surgery and six weeks in a cast followed by eight weeks in a walking boot. So far this time I have skipped surgery, had an air cast for six weeks, but was able to start walking without crutches at about three weeks, and am now spending six weeks in a lace-up brace that I can wear with or without my shoes on.

I know there are gifts that have happened during this break, too. I can't see them all yet (hindsight truly is better for some things) but I know the reorganizing of my autumn has brought gifts with it. One of them is that I no longer do the dishes or have much to do with the laundry. My older two girls have added that to their responsibilities.

As I heal more fully, I expect to start to realize the other gifts that have been given. Healing comes in many forms and sometimes we have to break something first.

PARENTING THE HIGHLY SENSITIVE

Not all of us are lucky enough to have perfectly healthy children leave our wombs or otherwise join our lives. Sometimes things go wrong and we don't get that "perfect" baby we were expecting.

Sometimes it appears that we did get that "perfect" baby, only to later find out that our child can't hear, wasn't born with social cues, or otherwise has a different brain.

Parenting takes on a whole new level when your child doesn't fall into "normal." And if you do have a "normal" child but choose to raise them differently (letting your boys cry or keep their hair long after toddlerhood or dressing your girls in gender-neutral clothes) you will get some of the evil side eye that every parent of a different child gets.

I am lucky. My daughters are by and large well within the range of "normal." Medically they are all good, and with the exception of my two reluctant readers (which seems better than saying late readers) are all within what you would expect, if not accelerated.

But I grew up with a brother who was premature, back when very few premature babies as small as he was survived. It is still pretty touch and go, even with all the advancements in technology, to have babies survive with his stats.

I grew up with my parents fighting for the Americans with Disability Act. You know the one that requires that street curbs have ramps for wheelchairs and strollers and crutches? It is the only activism I grew up with. I think I even wrote a letter to then First Lady Barbara Bush about it. I can't quite remember, just that we got a letter back. I grew up around kids with cerebral palsy, MS, in wheelchairs, severe dyslexia, deafness, and more things than I could probably name at the time. We lived on the same block as a house with an adult group home for the developmentally disabled. This was my normal, and the kids I played with outside of Girl Scouts either had these issues or were the siblings of children who had these issues. I can still spot if someone was born a preemie without them telling me; there is something about how their brain is wired differently that my subconscious picks up on.

My brother only had a 100-word vocabulary when he was 5 and I was 8 and trying to make my way in a new town and school. We got a lot of side eye at times. We walked to the park several times a week, especially once we were pulled out of school, and my mom would sit on the swing and read her book while we played. It was only as an adult that she shared with me that we often did that when she was having a hard day. Looking back with adult eyes, we went to the park a lot.

I don't know what it is like to raise a child with disabilities. I do know what it is like to raise four highly sensitive daughters who all react differently at parties, in crowds, and while we are shopping. I do know what it is like to spend hours and hours with children who are on the cusp of a major developmental leap but who just need to sit in the uncomfortableness of waiting. I have gotten side eye for having four daughters (even when they are behaving beautifully), for not having everyone reading excellently, for choosing our own course regarding sleepovers, tablets, Alexa, video games, movies, and the books we read.

I have friends who have children on the autism spectrum, children who are preemies, and whose children have changed gender. I don't know how many of the kids my kids interact with are on pharmaceutical drugs for behavior or moods, but I know some of them are. I do my best to support them and be there and listen, and love them regardless of who their children are. It is not always easy, because at times their children make no sense to the rest of the world. But I do my best to be there for the mom, because it's not her fault. And because so much of society doesn't give a damn.

And because those highly sensitive, differently wired and abled kids have so much joy to bring to our world. And so much to teach us.

All the Feels

Why Should I Be Responsible for Your Emotions?

We need to stop taking responsibility for our kids' emotions.

Seriously. They are themselves, their own beings that come into this world as their own selves.

We can't be responsible for how they feel.

In the beginning, the only way they can communicate with us is to cry, smile, and make little noises. They don't have the luxury of controlling their emotions at all, because that cry gets our attention so that we help them figure out what is going on. That smile rewards us for doing something right, for helping them feel contented and full of love.

I know this. I have held four babies in my arms and at times they have had to cry to get my attention. Not because I was in any way a neglectful parent, but because I have other children, a husband, and a very busy internal imagination, and maybe I just happened to be thinking of other things. Maybe, just maybe.

So how come at some point we feel like we have to take responsibility and be in charge of how our kids feel and therefore how they react? Is it the first time we can't get our baby to stop crying and we are either in public or are afraid that someone can hear us and therefore we will be judged?

Or maybe you're judging yourself because you don't actually like the sound of your baby crying and you feel ill-equipped to deal with it. Of course, we are biologically wired to feel uncomfortable when our baby cries - that is how it is supposed to work. Perhaps you are just so tired because it feels like this has been going on for days - and it may very well have been - and you are at your wits' end.

Somewhere in all of that you get to the point where you will do anything to just get your child to be happy again - most likely so you can get some more sleep, eat, or take a shower or go to the bathroom by yourself.

Then it snowballs. Your kid gets older and decides that the seat in the grocery store cart is electrified and they lose their shit. But you can't just walk out of the store because you actually need those groceries to be able to eat tonight.

Or your kid gets really angry at the other kid on the playground and hauls off and hits them and now they are banned from daycare.

Or your family is going through a really stressful shitty time and you don't know how to deal with your own emotions, much less deal with theirs. What they are feeling are totally valid and acceptable feelings, but they maybe aren't demonstrating them well, or they are lashing out at their safest person, which happens am doing the official camp training with Girl Scouts so I can take my troop camping when we are ready for that.

This means I am gone an extra amount of time right now. Oh, and we are pretty certain we are moving as well. So not only will I be leaving my children in my hubby's capable hands, but I will also be leaving the house in varying states of packing, and with that, the bigger mess that packing causes. I am not sure what else I can do right now and I have been really clear about what is going on. My eldest goes on her camping trip with her troop the weekend after we close, which may end up being the weekend we move everything. Again, this is how things work sometimes.

I am surprised how hard my leaving is hitting my 6-year-old. She cried and cried all the way home a week ago when she found out that my retreat was this week. I have been trying not to bring it up around her too much so she can just enjoy life and not spend a lot of time worrying about what is coming.

She can't give me any solid reasons why she doesn't want me to go. She really doesn't have to. The fact that our life is in turmoil with house buying hell is enough of a reason to not want any change in her routine. Knowing that her Dad is much more spontaneous than I am and is less likely to have a schedule and a plan for the day could be harder for her to deal with, since she is used to her Virgo sister getting the plan from me and sharing it.

I am grateful that I leave early in the morning so that our goodbyes are tonight and not when I then need to drive for two hours. It will be harder the next two times I leave because it will be in the late to be you, much like you took your shit out on your partner or best friend last week.

Yet knowing all this, you still give the stink eye to another parent whose kid is losing their shit. Maybe it's on an airplane, maybe they are throwing a fit in the checkout line, or maybe it's just not-great behavior at the umpteenth birthday party you have had to attend this weekend (hint: you can say no, you don't have to go to all of them).

We do, though - we judge each other on how our kids are behaving, even though we are not in complete control of them, and we most certainly are not in control of their feelings. Hell, half the time we are not in control of our own.

But does any of this judging actually help our kids or change the situation? Sometimes your kid just needs to cry, because yes, as far as they are concerned, not getting the green popsicle instead of the red one is the end of the world and something they need to grieve over. Because they had wrapped a whole story up in their mind about how much cooler the green popsicle would make them look.

We don't know. Frankly, I don't want to be in my kids' minds. Mine is hard enough to control and listen to constantly as it is - hence why we invented meditation, alcohol, and binge-worthy TV. I don't live in their bodies or understand how their brain rewired itself last night (and new research shows it probably did).

Why do I have to be responsible for their emotions?

I am responsible to my kids to be the best mum I can be. I am not responsible for their behavior. I'm responsible to keep them as safe as I can, but at some point they may still make stupid decisions and it's my job to be there to help them pick up the pieces and fix it.

I will not take my kids' feelings away from them. I will try and help them find ways of processing how they feel without harming others or destroying friendships they don't want to destroy. But it is not my fault that my child is having a bad time and feels miserable, or conversely is having an awesome day.

All I can control is my reactions to them. I can create safe environments for them to learn what the world wants to teach them. Their lessons are not my lessons to learn, necessarily. My lesson is how to help support them to get through theirs.

Because that's my job as their mum.

SHE'S CRYING AGAIN

She is crying again and I don't know why. She is crying so hard that when I ask her what's wrong all I can make out is one or two words in her whole sentence.

It's the snotty filled kind of crying where her whole body shakes with the force of her tears. I don't think she is hurt physically, I think this is emotional pain.

Once again I don't know what I am supposed to do. Our culture doesn't teach us what to do to when someone is crying, beyond rubbing their back and hoping that they stop soon. So much so that as parents we will do just about anything to get a child to stop crying in public for fear that everyone will be looking at us and judging us for the fact that our kiddo is crying.

But none of that is really any help. Yes, we want our child to know that we are there for them when they are crying (though maybe we don't really feel there when we are the one that caused the crying because we have emotions and get angry and pissed off too) but often we can't fix it.

Especially not when they are sobbing so hard we can't understand what they are saying.

Lately I have been trying to just be there for them. Just hold them if they want a hug (and I am not in the middle of cooking on the stove where they might have to wait a minute until I can get to a stopping point) and just be there next to them until they can calm down enough to tell me what is going on. If they want to – I understand that as my daughters get older they may not always want to tell me why they are crying.

Holding the space for their emotions is difficult. Having to hold space for my own emotions feels much harder. I was raised mainly to be Vulcan, so even identifying my emotions outside of happiness can be hard.

I remember how shocked and then ashamed I was after my first daughter was born. She was only a couple of days old and my mother (who was staying with us to help out) and my hubby sent me to take a nap because I was exhausted. I was asleep for less than a half hour when they woke me up to nurse my daughter. I was so angry at this little baby for waking me up after I felt I had only just fallen asleep. I swear I saw red. I was so mad. And then immediately I felt so ashamed at being mad at this small person, who only wanted to nurse and be cuddled by her mum. I made sure to have breastmilk in the fridge in the future so that I could get a nap in every now and then. But the point remains that for years I was ashamed at how mad I had gotten at my newborn.

Emotions just *are*. If you shove them down or try to ignore them they just get bigger or come out sideways in the end. As a society we see this with anger management classes and with the acknowledgement that grief looks different for everyone. But we don't really know how to support others, or what to do to help them.

I think sometimes the simplest answer and the best place to start is to just sit with the person. Whether they are a baby or in their 90s, sitting next to them, or holding them if that's your relationship, is the best place to start. Hold space for them to feel their emotions and not be alone while they are feeling them. Be there to bear witness to the fact that their feelings are valid.

My eldest was amazing last summer. One of her favorite ducks ended up passing away while we were out of town visiting relatives. Her Dad had to break the news to me and then I had to break the news to her. She cried solidly for about 10 minutes and then she was done. This doesn't mean that her grief was done and that she doesn't still talk about missing this particular duck. But the full-body emotional reaction to his death was able to be processed in about 10 minutes and then she was able to move on to telling stories about all the things she loved about him and going back out to play.

I envy her ability to do that. I often feel like crying but can't. I am working through that and trying to find more opportunities to cry. But it is often hard. I think some of it comes from being "on duty" as a parent to my kids most of the time, since they are with me most of the time. While intellectually I don't have a problem with them seeing me cry, I cannot always explain to them the reasons why I am crying and I often worry that a parent crying without a reason they can explain to their child (though maybe just saying I am sad works) would be scary.

I know that blowing up in anger can be scary.

My girls and I are currently working on creating playlists for emotions. Here's my pissed–off playlist full of songs for when I am pissed off, so I can dance out my emotions. Here's one for anger. I created one for heartbreak a long time ago.

Playlists for happiness, sadness, jealousy, and fear probably all need to be created too. It's a work in progress, just like we are.

CREATING THE GAP IN EMOTIONS

My youngest is full of energy. Years ago we would have said she was full of spunk, was ornery, or is just a little shit. Everyone would immediately know what I was talking about. She's the kid who had her first full–blown temper tantrum because I refused to allow her to take the crib mattress as a sled down our stairs and straight into the wall. She was only about two years old when this happened.

She is the kid that will just slap a sister out of the blue for some remembered slight that happened. She's the kid that the moment she walks into a room you know she is there. One of her middle names means "the great queen" and by golly she knows it.

She is the embodiment of a strong-willed child. You know the one where the memes tell you to hang in there? Yeah, well, in this day and age there is not as much support.

If you have a strong-willed child, especially if they are not afraid to express their emotions that are not socially acceptable (so pretty much anything other than happiness), there is not a lot of support. I am pretty sure if she went to preschool these days she would already have the label of bully. Not because she is a bully, but because, you know, she tries everything on, even dictating.

Why? Because she's a kid and she's still learning. Because she came into this world ready to change it, whether the world is ready for her or not. Because one of her special gifts is the ability to advocate, and she is learning to not just do it for herself but for others as well.

Case in point, last night my hubby and I were packing up a bookcase and the younger two were being the gofers of the books and then the full boxes going back on the book case until we are ready to move. At some point my 6-year-old got really upset about something her Dad said. As near as we can tell, she misunderstood something and thought he was laughing at her, when in actuality he wasn't. Because at that point in time I couldn't stop to cuddle her and find out what was going on, her little sister did. I saw them cuddling on the couch with my 6-year-old whispering what was wrong in my 4-year-old's ear and them going back and forth and snuggling.

Which is frigging awesome for the girl that randomly slapped her sister only the night before.

We are under a lot of stress right now. House buying does that to a person, which was not something I realized before we were neck deep into the process. None of us are functioning at our best right now. While sometimes I get filled with Mommy guilt, because I know I am not doing my best at the moment, I also know that how we react now, in times where things aren't easy, are just as important as the easy-going days.

A friend helped support me with my youngest and recommended a couple of flower essences that might help her feel better. After I ordered them and they arrived, I explained them to my four-year-old by saying, "This one is for when you feel like being really mean, and this one is for when you feel super grumpy and don't want to be around anyone. This one is for when you are having trouble going to sleep." After a few weeks, amazing things have started happening.

She now comes to me with the flower essence bottle and asks if she can have some because she is feeling whatever the emotion is that I suggested the bottle might help with. Her reading skills are still at the letter recognition stage, but each bottle has a different picture of the flower on it, so she can tell them apart.

Regardless of whether you think flower essences work, they are still creating a lovely gap. My four-year-old feels a big emotion and realizes she needs help. She is able to identify the emotion enough to grab the bottle she wants (and she doesn't always grab the same one – she is very intentional about which one she grabs) and bring it to me and then verbally tell me how she is feeling.

I then give her four drops on her tongue. Sometimes she wants to stay and talk about what is going on, but often she just says "thank you" and takes the bottle to put back where it goes and gets on with her day.

It just amazes me that she is a) identifying how she is feeling b) realizing it is too big for her and she needs to get some help c) going and getting the thing that might help her d) finding an adult to help her get the thing and e) able to tell the adult how she is feeling.

There are some adults who still can't manage this process. But here is my four-year-old, creating a gap between how she feels and her response to how she feels. Obviously it isn't perfect yet (hence the random acts of violence) but we are getting there. Teaching her brain to pause is going to bring so much good juiciness in the future. The acknowledgment of the feelings and having someone else witness her feelings (which in turn validates them) is incredible. As is the fact that she is learning ways to deal with them herself and that is also empowering.

WAITING FOR THEM TO GET OVER IT

I am waiting for them to get used to this huge adjustment.

We closed on our house on the 13th, and it's now the 28th. It took us 10 days, until the 23rd, to finish getting everything out of the old house and clean it up. So now we are completely in this new house, and have been for about four days.

Of course it is still a chaotic disaster. My hubby and I spent our time off doing the actual moving, and now we are both back to needing to keep up with our work.

There is still about two rooms' worth of stuff outside in the driveway waiting to go down in the basement, and it has rained three or four times now.

I have a table set up in my office, but things are still strewn all over it. My kids don't yet recognize that if my door is shut it means I'm unavailable.

I am only doing the bare minimum of work so that I have time to do other things, like unpack boxes and take my kids to summer activities so I can run away from the unpacking of the boxes.

I am hosting an unpacking party next Monday. Right now there just looks to be three of us. I am still hoping that will help us get over the edge and have more things unpacked and put away than still in boxes. Every time I try to put things away I get interrupted and distracted by all the other things I find along the way.

My girls are still clingy. My almost-5-year-old has regressed to about 3, most of the time, with the occasional glimmer of 5 in her speech. Her need to be attached to my hip got old about a week ago. Of course, a week ago I was still making runs back and forth between the two houses and therefore had built in-breaks. Now they are back to being with me 24/7.

Instead of just chillaxing this weekend, my hubby and I have to take care of the insulation in the basement that we were going to do the day we closed. Due to a whole comedy of errors, including getting locked out of one of our cars, we decided not to do it then and instead to just get out of the rental as soon as possible. I believe that made our landlords happy as they are trying to get their new tenants in by the first and not have any interruptions in rent.

My kids are whining about wanting to go to the playground and the beach, and I am not familiar enough with our new rural neighborhood to know much more than where the library is, and we only found that on Monday. I just want to get things unpacked and have a few minutes to read my book.

Also, did you know your kids could get tired of eating hamburgers, like that was even possible? Yeah, I didn't know that either.

My kitchen is a mess. My hubby and I need to set it up, and we just haven't had the time. I guess we need to do that tonight because it's Thursday and starting Friday night we will be working in the basement until that job is done, which is hopefully sooner rather than later.

I think I have found most of our DVD's, at least the kid ones. They had fit the gaps in the book boxes really well, and I have a lot of those unpacked, although not all of them because the clips for the last three bookcase shelves have decided to walk away, or something. I spent way too much time yesterday trying to find them, only to have them not appear. The little bastards.

I am still not sure how the spare box of cat litter ended up in my office. I think it's going to end up in the basement for when we need it under tires or something. We totally have the cat on something else now, and she mainly goes outside, thank the cat goddesses.

No one has vomited or puked yet, though we have had some upset tummies and two cases of people not making it to the bathroom on time.

I know that this is a phase and it will pass, and I am trying my damnedest to be patient. Really I am.

But that magic Mary Poppins cleaning up thing, that would be wonderful right about now. Absolutely wonderful.

CHILDHOOD FRIENDSHIPS

I was convinced growing up that I wasn't any good at making friends. My family moved a lot, not because I was an army brat (which might actually have been easier since there seems to be the opportunity for a lot of support for military families and their moves), just because that was how life worked for my parents.

When you only live in a place three or four years at a time, you make friends, but they don't come with you when you move. This being before the internet and social media, you would literally lose track of the person. It was like you walked out of their life and into a new one.

There are upsides to that. You can change your name if you want, or get rid of any hideous nicknames. You can vary how you introduce yourself. You can change your story slightly.

But the times we moved that I recall best, I was no longer in school, so I didn't automatically make friends there. With homeschooling, it was harder than that. Also, being a one-car family whose one car was not very reliable meant that playdates were never something that happened very often.

So I was convinced by the time I was 18 that even though I'd had a boyfriend for almost a year before dumping him, that I really wasn't any good at making friends. I even thought I sucked at it. Of course, once I started working as a camp counselor and having more control over my life, that changed. Now, after having lived in Maine for almost eight years, I have some deep friendships.

Our next door neighbors have three kids. Twin 10-year-olds (a boy and a girl) and an older daughter who's got to be in (or just about in) high school. My kids love to play with the younger daughter as much as they can around her school, sports, and homework schedule. Which basically means that my kids are always wanting to know if today is a school day, if it's after the time that school gets out, and if the above is true, if they can go knock on the neighbors' door.

More often than not they get rejected. More often than not, even if the neighbor girl can come to play, it won't be for very long and something will call her away. But my kids seem to be infinite optimists and will keep asking until hell freezes over or we move.

Which we are doing. As the lawyers and realtors and bankers discuss closing two days sooner, it all seems even more likely that this deal will go through and we will be moving in about two weeks. The new neighbors, who we haven't met but who have seen our kids, have girls around the ages of my older two, and so the sellers guess there is going to be a path worn between our two houses.

Of course that doesn't mean the kids will even like each other. And who knows how the other parents parent, cause you know that can throw a spanner in the works if their parenting style is too different from our own. But there could be some new automatic friendships.

My girls are all staying in their Girl Scout troops, so none of that is changing, and we will actually be closer to some of our family friends we have made here in Maine, so it will be easier to get together with them. But my kids still worry. I get that. I get the wondering and the hoping and being unsure. It is a much smaller community we are moving into, with between 1,000 and 1,500 residents depending on who you ask, so while we will spend some time hanging out at the library (which is often a good place to make new friends) this is a period of transition and it will take a while for everyone to feel comfortable again.

I don't think all my kids think that they are awful at making friends like I did. My 9-year-old seems to easily make friends and is often the peacekeeper in her Girl Scout troop. My 11-year-old may feel that making friends is hard, and like me, might be trying to find friendships that are similar to what you read about in books, even though those friendships are not the same as we can make in real life.

My 4-year-old just decides if she likes you or not and then you are her friend, and my 6-year-old is also pretty easy-going. All four of them get stuck hanging out with family friends from time to time, though we do try and make that as painless as possible.

It's not like there are any guidebooks to making friends, and if they were it doesn't mean the other person has read it.

SUPER BIG EMOTIONS

Lately my normally mellow six-year-old has had some super big emotions, mainly around fairness and when she doesn't think things are fair. But they can come out of nowhere.

Right now we are in the two-month period where my other three daughters all have birthdays. From August to October we have three birthdays, and of course my 6-year-old was born in January, which feels ages and ages away when you are only six.

Plus we live in the northern hemisphere where there are things like snow, so grandmothers never come to visit for the January birthday, and for the last three years we have had a grandmother visiting for at least one of my other three daughters' birthdays.

This is just not fair. It really isn't. But there also isn't much I can do about it. As someone who was born three days after Christmas, I still feel like my birthdays suck, because who really wants to go to another party between Christmas and New Years? Plus it means I only get gifts at one time of the year and they are often combined or people are stretched thin because of all the gift-giving at Christmas. So I get it. It does truly suck.

But at the same time, what am I as her mother supposed to do to help? I can't very well do a half-birthday for her in the summer and have it actually work in terms of spending less money, because she is not old enough to understand putting off what she wants for a while (I mean who is, really?).

And she really doesn't truly want consolation right now, I think. Yes, she tells me she wants the feelings to go away, and I offer suggestions, like tapping, or flower essences. When I am not facing the situation head-on, I can think of things like maybe she needs to dance it out, go for a walk, or make some art around it.

I will try to keep those ideas in mind the next time it happens - because of course now that I am writing this it isn't happening right this second, though it was when I started this essay, but it is now several days later before I have gotten back to it because such is life as a mother.

But I don't know that I will remember. As much as I work hard to stay calm during these emotional storms that are not my own, some days I do better than others.

I think there is supposed to be some work around *acknowledging my own emotions helps my kids acknowledge theirs*, but sometimes it doesn't seem like a very safe option. We are often told not to lose our shit while our kid is spreading their shit all over the world. We are supposed to try and stay calm and collected so our kids feel safe to spread that shit. However I wonder, as we get older, who holds that space for us?

Who do we get to vent to who will not hold it against us but will instead hold space for us? It feels like as an adult, someone is always judging us, and we are not supposed to share all our secrets with the world lest someone decide to hold it over us later.

There is certainly behavior that does have severe consequences, regardless of what the good old boys would have us believe. But so much of learning, of understanding how to get around in our world and our lives, is around making mistakes.

Mistakes must be made. They must be experienced for the lessons to be learned, and yet as adults, many of us feel shame around those mistakes and no one wants to admit to feeling shame. No one at all.

Which gets me back to holding space while my child is raging. What may be mere seconds feels like hours and hours and since we are not in charge of the emotion it can feel like it will take forever for them to move past it. My 6-year-old has brought up this unfairness multiple times in the last week, so I do not feel like she has fully processed the emotion yet. She still seems to be in the thick of it.

Where is the guidebook? We are supposed to just sit and hold them and maybe rub their back, right? And eventually the emotion will shift and they will move on. That is how it is supposed to work.

Just like eventually they won't need to touch base with us every fucking second they are awake. It moves to every minute, five, ten, and then sometimes occasionally they can go an hour without touching base with me.

I hear that when they have left home it may even be longer than that. I wonder what that will be like.

CREATIVE CHAOS

It's a week until we close on our new house. We are not getting movers to help us. We might be getting some local teenage boys who we can pay and buy soda and pizza for on the weekend, and possibly a friend with a pick-up truck, but by and large we are doing it ourselves.

We have play-dates for the girls scheduled for the actual closing and the evening afterward, so we can fix a few things in the basement, and then for the first day at the new place. My 9-year-old and I plan to start bringing things down from the attic this afternoon and start staging that in the office. Eventually it would be nice to have everything moved downstairs so it's just a matter of emptying that first floor and the yard, and moving ducks and hops.

I am gone this weekend for two nights and parts of 3 days. I am looking forward to getting away from all the chaos for a while and just having to worry about me. Not to mention the 3-and-a-half-hour drive and all the audiobook listening I will get done in that period.

I chose not to go on my long walk this morning because I am planning on doing all those stairs and moving stuff out of the attic. I don't know if I will get it all moved down today or if I will start running out of steam before we finish. Plus we will have to see how it goes with the stacking skills of the 9-year-old.

We got our closing statement yesterday, which means we know the exact amount of money we need to bring to closing, and it's a lot less than the loan estimate. Which means we will have some money left over, which means we can probably improve the septic system this year rather than waiting until after tax return time next year. That is pretty exciting, but it also means more chaos when they are actually there installing the new tank.

I still need to call and cancel our renters, umbrella, and car insurance as that is all being bundled over with our homeowners' insurance starting next week. We will be saving money, but for some reason I haven't gotten to calling the insurance yet. That has to be done today, as well as writing to our garbage people and letting them know we won't be needing them after this month.

Meanwhile the girls are needing a lot more touch right now, lots of cuddles, uppy, and otherwise hugs and hand-holding. So far our schedule has remained much the same. I get work done for my business on weekday mornings, this is the second-to-last week of Girl Scout meetings, and we are still reading Harry Potter at breakfast though we are two chapters away from finishing *The Order of the Phoenix* and all that brings.

We are still watching an episode or two of YouTube at night as a family or taking walks. It has been raining for the last three days, but since that means clearer weather for both my camping trip and moving next week, we are happy to deal with the rain now.

Meals are beginning to get a bit crazy as I am not restocking the freezer, partially because I have been out of town on the weekends lately when the really good sales are, and partially because it will be one less thing to move in the pantry. I was able to buy a bunch of discounted but still good ground beef last week and got it all divided and frozen up, and that has been really helpful in this transition period.

I am grateful to soon not have to be dealing with landlords anymore. To be working toward having all my girls sleeping back in their own rooms instead of showing up at the end of the bed each night. I am grateful to be able to set up my new office fairly quickly so that since I often try and get my writing done before my girls wake up, I won't be trying to do it around the girls sleeping at the end of our bed.

I am getting frustrated, though. I know that in some ways a week is not a lot of time, but in other ways it feels like we are all ready so we should just be able to go. We even have the day before closing pretty well planned out, with an ice cream social end-of-the-year

Daisy Girl Scout party, probably followed by driving out for a games night at a friend's house to say goodbye to another friend who is moving out to Wyoming. That should help us sleep that final night, and we both have the next five days off to do closing and move most of our stuff.

I did that on my own last time, most of the moving, with just maybe one run of help from my hubby at night. Now I will be doing it with him, so not only will we need to be working together, but we will also be releasing a lot of the stress that has built up for the past few months while going through this home-buying process and that is bound to come out sideways a few times. I am going to work hard to keep my temper from exploding, but we will see. Lots of physical labor can bring out the worst in people sometimes.

Each day seems to require more and more creative parenting, as the girls are trying to process their feelings without really understanding what is going on and not really enjoying it either. The fighting and sniping with each other has increased, and some days I just want to scream "Shut the fuck up!" But I don't, because the consequences of that is everyone crying, and I am trying to make this process as seamless as possible.

I envy the Coast Guard wives that are leaving at the same time. I am sure they have done the moving thing so often that they have it down to a science. I also know that other parts of the military help each other out and actually do the moving and unpacking for you once you get there. That seems like a bit of heaven today.

But we will get there, and we will get it done, and it will have ups and downs, but the ups at the end of it will outweigh the downs. The chaos will go back towards order a bit.

THE BABIES THAT DON'T GET BORN

We don't talk about them, do we? The babies that don't get born, or the ones that do but weren't still alive or died so quickly afterward.

We just don't talk about them. We pretend that they didn't happen.

Until we see something on social media. Or we see someone else brave enough to talk about their pregnancy loss. And then it hits us in the gut again.

The lost ones.

I don't fit into the normal miscarriage story. Or at least I don't feel like I do. But maybe I am being too harsh on myself.

When I was pregnant for the first time with my firstborn, I remember thinking that my hubby and mother were way more excited than I was. I was well, sick. Morning sickness was a bitch, and since my mother didn't have it, she wasn't a lot of help. Midwives don't really want to see you too much until you are near the end of your first trimester, so we had an interview appointment and then waited another month for an actual appointment.

I told my manager at the fabric store, because I wanted her to know in case I looked as green as I felt. But I didn't tell the rest of the world until after we made it through that first trimester, because that is what you do, right?

Because what if you lose the baby? You don't want to tell the whole world, right? This was the very beginning of 2006 so everyone wasn't on Facebook yet and I never bothered with MySpace. I had only had a cell phone for a few years anyway.

Then in February my hubby, who worked at a mass retailer who I can't name, hurt his back while moving one microwave from a shelf to another shelf. It wasn't listed as a team lift but something about the twisting action caused (we later found out) two herniated discs. This was February. I was at work. My hubby got taken to the ER and he wouldn't let me come because I was pregnant and he didn't want to expose me to all the hospital germs. My mother met him there. They waited over 7 hours to get seen. He still doesn't know how he managed to sit there, but suspects it was an out-of-body experience.

I cried a lot that weekend. It felt like our world was collapsing around us and he would never get better and there was so much he now wasn't able to do. It was a workman's comp issue, so I couldn't even take him to a chiropractor or it would void the workman's comp.

I remember during the course of that weekend thinking that I had lost our baby. But at the next midwife visit a few weeks later, we heard our baby's heartbeat for the first time.

Fast forward to September 2006, when my first daughter was born. I am not going to tell her birth story here, just the bit that happened afterward. Because I delivered her at a birth center with midwives that were actively teaching other midwives, they examined my placenta. They got quite excited about it because it was an "elephant ear" placenta, where there were two connection points.

Let me say that again. There were two connection points.

Which means at one point or another I had been carrying two embryos. I *had* lost our baby in February.

Now I am grateful we didn't have twins, don't get me wrong. I thought twins sounded great until I became a parent, and now I am so grateful that I have only ever had one child at a time.

I don't know how we would have handled two at once, especially since we couldn't have had a midwife delivery.

So I am sure it was for the best.

But...

But...

That missing child still haunts my husband and I. We still think about them. We often wonder if that was our son, the boy we never had. Sometimes we miss them, and wonder who they are. We sometimes joke that our youngest is the spirit child of my first pregnancy because she is so close to our eldest (and different in a lot of ways). But we don't know.

We don't tell this story much. Only to a few close friends. Maybe my eldest absorbed the other twin? We don't really know. I know that my eldest has always understood the darkness and avoided it more than any of my other children, and my youngest likes to play there.

We don't talk about pregnancy loss.

But it happens all the time.

Chances are it has happened to someone you know, if not you. Yet we ignore it, and shove it under the rug.

Like a shadow we can't face.

But the thing about shadows is that they grow when you try and hide them. We are better off acknowledging them, sharing their stories and maybe even occasionally setting a place at the table for them.

Because part of us always wonders

What if...........?

I'm Not *Just* A Parent!

Coming and Going

Going and coming, we are like tides in the lives of our children. We are always either coming or going, because when we are actually there, when we are staying with them, we just become those pieces of things taken for granted, that safety, that security that *everything will be fine because my mother is here.*

It is only when we have to leave, when we have to have a few minutes of time to ourselves, or go and work at our job, or any other reason, that suddenly they realize how much they need us, because now we are gone. We are that firm foundation that they are attached to because they grew inside of us or because we have become their living breathing security blanket, because we are their everything and often they can not really see us as separate from them. When we go it is like a major earthquake in their lives.

The ground beneath their feet shifts. Even if this happens all the time at scheduled intervals. Even if we have warned them ahead of time. Even if they are staying with family or friends or doing something they really truly enjoy, we are still leaving them, in their minds. Every single time.

I have been the full-time working parent and I have been the default stay-at-home *what do you mean you would ever leave me?* parent.

I have been both of those things and honestly they both have lovely shit sandwiches to eat. I don't think either is better than the other. They all hurt when you need to walk away when you are going.

And the coming back. When you come back from being away, whether it was for half an hour or three days, there is always much that needs to be done. Hugs and kisses, lots of talking and snuggling. Or if you have a preteen or teenager, lots of the silent treatment while they let you know that they didn't appreciate you were gone by ignoring you when you come back.

Meanwhile you might need to reconnect with your partner. If you are a single mom there is probably at least a caretaker you need to check in with. Or they may be so excited to leave that it feels a bit like bringing the baby home from the hospital and now suddenly you are abandoned and alone with this child(ren).

It can feel like it takes a while for your kids to settle back in, to trust that you are staying home (and maybe you aren't able to stay at home for a while, maybe you do have work the next day or another reason to be away at night or on a weekend). It takes so much longer than you think it will take.

They become clingy or grumpy or just turn up every time you turn around and need your attention. It can make the your transition back to daily life a little harder than you were expecting. Especially if you are tired, as traveling often makes us more tired than we expect no matter how many times we do it.

But from your kid's perspective, it is all about them, because that is what they need to be like to ensure their survival to adulthood. And you just left them. Even if it was only to run to the grocery store for 30 minutes, you just abandoned them.

They are not impressed. This is not something they gave their approval for, even if they didn't want to go and do the thing you needed to do anyway (and honestly, I think they probably would rather come and hang with you and drive you crazy because what you are doing is boring *rather* than being left at home or away from you). Unless you can schedule a wonderful playdate with their best friend, but even then they may not be that happy for you to go, or are annoyed that you came back and are ending their playdate.

But this is the reality of life. We for our sanity and ease and because sometimes we do not have any other choice, need to go and be away from our kids. And then we need to come back. This dance of comings and goings, we dance it with each child. We dance it as a family.

It can be intricate and we can feel like we never learned the steps, but the dance is going to happen whether we want it to or not, whether or not we feel confident in our steps. At the end of the day we need to find ways to acknowledge how we all feel and make space for those feelings and then come back together to all feel safer and closer and safer.

MARRIAGE IS HARD

Everyone tells you this, but most of the time when you are engaged or newly wed you just brush it off. Like "that is what it is like for everyone else, but me and my soulmate, we are special. It's not going to be hard for us. We are going to rock this marriage thing. It's going to be just fine."

Then of course you start having conflicts, or fights, and things don't go your way. You're sleep-deprived, or hungry, or you've just had a great disappointment and you're upset. You speak to your partner like you would a girlfriend, or an enemy, and things just start to fall apart. Especially once you introduce children. Because they have their own needs and demands and often when they are small they have to come first, and the time you have for yourself or your partnership disappears and when you do get to that long-awaited date or time when the baby has fallen asleep you are so tired that you can't even see straight, let alone have a meaningful conversation or muster enough energy to get romantically involved. And that sucks.

No one really talks about it. You're not supposed to talk about it because that would be admitting that marriage is in fact hard. We don't want to admit that there are rough patches and that just like your children who you love with all your heart, you can love your partner and yet at the same time be so angry at them you see red.

So what do you do? Eventually you have to make up, or apologize, or walk away from the relationship.

Those are really the only options. I think in most relationships, one person is going to be the one to apologize or to try and fix the situation first. It is usually the same person, which ends up not feeling very healthy and can be one-sided. *Why do I always have to be the one to apologize first? What happens if I wait for him to make it better? Why is the wife always right? Why should I have to bring her flowers/candy/jewelry?*

We are not usually given conflict-resolution tools. We are not taught what to do when our emotions get the best of us around the people we love, and our emotions will get the best of us from time to time. Not to mention if anyone has an injury. Chronic pain or just the pain from an injury can put a whole new spin on the relationship. Things you used to rely on the other person doing may have to be things that you need to do. You may not be as proficient at it or care about it as much as the other person, but you still have to do it. That too causes resentment.

These patterns of conflict and how you resolve them can loom large. They say a relationship is more than the sum of the people involved. It takes on a life of its own. I would wager that part of that life of its own has to do with the fact that how you deal with conflict becomes a pattern and a story and we all want to be the hero in it and we all want to follow the paths we have followed before.

We care deeply about this person, so we don't want to fight with them (or maybe we do because that is how we learned to get attention in the first place) and we want to get back to knowing that they love and respect us and that we are the sun and moon to them (though that may not be completely healthy).

What do you do when someone gets angry? Especially when it may just be because they had a bad night's sleep or they are super hungry, or they are on a diet or making a major lifestyle change. What do you do when you come home at night and one person hogs the conversation about their day and doesn't seem to ask about yours? How do you learn to take turns and navigate hurt feelings? How do you create a safe container in which to say what you need to say and be truly heard so that you can find a path forward together?

Marriage is hard. It takes work. Not just the day to day picking up after yourself shit, or taking care of the other person when they are sick. In some ways, being there for the other person while they are grieving a loss of a loved one or an opportunity or healing from an injury can take more work than looking after them when they are sick.

You have to figure out when they need space, when you need space, and when it's the right time to come back together and what that looks like for your relationship. Perhaps taking turns starting the resolution process is the best way to go about it. Perhaps not mouthing off about the other person to someone else is a good way to keep the relationship moving the way you want it to. Perhaps just finding the time and space to reconnect is the most important. Knowing that that time is always there, and having it regularly show up on your schedule, is the most important thing you can do to help conflict-proof your marriage.

Do You Talk to Your Partner Enough?

I am not about to tell you what is going to work for you and your partner. But I know from experience that when I don't make time for my relationship with my hubby, everything goes to shit. Literally and figuratively.

It can be so easy to just let things slide. To not take turns sharing how your day went, letting the kids' needs and schedules come before your own. To not go out on a date or ask for what you need or turn the TV off with enough time to spare to actually say *hi* to this person who is on this journey with you.

I have felt just as selfish asking for time and money to go on a date with my spouse as I have felt about spending time and money on myself. My hubby and I have come up with some really creative ways to go on "dates" without actually having to leave our kids or get a babysitter.

Lately reading aloud a shared book at night has created a good connection between the two of us and is a great way to wind down and get ready to sleep.

But it is not easy. It is not easy to keep showing up with our vulnerable heart in our hands and share.

Esther Perel has helped. Brené Brown has helped more than she can imagine. Friends have helped by watching our kids and letting us sneak away, or being a safe ear when we have needed to work things out.

We had a wonderful marriage counselor in a time of crisis. We have kept our parents out of our relationship by and large, because that has worked for us. We regularly make time to be just us.

But it is hard. Sometimes I don't want to have another uncomfortable conversation. I don't want to have to share how I am feeling, I just want to be pissed off. I certainly don't always want to be the first to apologize.

But I do. We both do. Because at the end of the day, the kids will all have left home and it will just be us. As we tell our daughters all the time about their relationships with each other, at the end of the day it will just be them and it will just be us and you have to make sure those relationships stay strong.

Is this something we always have worked out? Hell no. It's like parenting; just when we think we have it figured out, the rules change. The situation changes. We change. But would I want to take this ride with anyone else?

No. Which is why my relationship with my partner comes first. Right after my relationship with myself and right before my relationship with all of my girls.

Do you feel like you talk to your partner enough?

TRIALS OF MOMPRENEUR LIFE

Yesterday I had a conference call with my virtual assistant, because not as much would get done around here for the Mommy Rebellion if I did not have a virtual assistant.

Luckily, Lisa is also a mom, to a 7-year-old son, so she gets it. Her son goes to school, so she is able to schedule our calls while he is busy. Me, however? I have kids with me 24/7 most days and my youngest (at not quite 5) has really been pushing the boundaries lately.

She was literally pushing buttons yesterday, or rather sticking her feet in my face during the end of our conference call. I have photographic proof.

One the one hand, it was great that Lisa was able to snap a photo for me, because it will make for great marketing materials for the Mommy Rebellion. Just about every mom can relate to that photo. But on the other hand, gosh darn it, why can't she stay out of my office for 30 minutes?

I am going to have to start leaving the house to get my work done. I have tried locking the door and that has led to her practically breaking it down. While my husband is okay if she does break the door down and is okay with me keeping it locked, it does get very distracting, both for me and the other people on the video call.

I swear it was easier when she was two. She got to watch TV with her big sisters and I made sure she had a snack and was all set to go while I was on a call. Nowadays, forget it!

So the ultimate solution is for me to just leave. My eldest is old enough to babysit. She's not going to like it and will get annoyed if it becomes a regular thing. But I am guessing I am only going to have to do it a time or two before my youngest gets the picture and stops being such a pain. Of course, moving to a new town, and a more rural one at that, I am actually not sure where I can go and have wifi access, which is usually what I need while working. I mean I can do a little, like writing this, without wifi access, but I can not do things for my clients without it.

I don't want to do it. I don't want to have that big confrontation and just leave. But this interrupting, not letting me get my work done, and all around disrespect of my work time can't stand either. It's not fair to me, it's not fair to my clients, and it is not fair to her either, because she needs to learn limits.

Plus, we are only talking about three hours a day. She can manage to not really need me much for three hours a day. She has three older sisters to interact with. Right now she has a visiting grandmother and uncle (which is why I didn't just leave this morning) to hang out with as well. I spend the rest of the day with her.

I drive her places. We play games. I make sure she has food. I read to her and her sisters. I really think that her needs are being met and that at almost 5 she can do without me for three hours a day, four days a week. That's all I'm asking for.

I would get so much more done! Not having the constant interruptions would mean that I would get a lot more done at any given time than I do right now, because I could just focus, rather than being torn away and then having to come back and remember where I am and refocus.

You know what I mean, right?

Plus, while it was funny this time, I really don't want to conduct meetings with feet in my face. It's not like they are super cute and yummy newborn feet. These are sweaty, dirty, stinky big girl feet that do not need to be in my face. Ever. Especially not when I am conducting a meeting and trying to get work done.

I don't want to have that in my vocabulary any more. I don't want to say I am *trying* to get work done. I want to say I am working. I am getting work done. Work is happening. I am pursuing my dreams and supporting my clients and growing Mommy Rebellion. I am writing. I am creating.

I am tired of being held hostage by the interrupting chickens. They created locks on the doors for reasons. I am going to get a treadmill desk in the next year. This is happening. I need to walk and do my work with minimal interruptions, especially during meetings.

She will survive. I will actually want to spend MORE time with her because she won't have been interrupting me all morning and I will have actually gotten some work DONE instead of having it bleed into time I would normally be spending with her because she used up my work time.

Yep, it could all be so much easier.

I'd better find out where those wifi spots are, eh?

GOING ON RETREAT

Twice a year I leave my girls.

I go to a business retreat that in the beginning lasted two days and now lasts three days, so I am gone for two nights.

I do this about every six months.

The first time I went to the retreat, which is usually about an hour and a half from my house, I actually drove home for the night between the two days. It was exhausting, since I needed to be there at 9 am the next day.

Ever since then I have stayed either with friends or shared hotel rooms with other people at my retreat.

This week I leave again, and my parents have come to town to stay home with the kids, instead of my husband having to take time off of work.

While my youngest is now four and no longer a nursling, it is still bittersweet to walk away from my kids for three days. They always grow while I am away and their vocabularies get bigger (I swear) and they have so very much to say and....

Meanwhile, at my retreat we do a lot of inner and outer work, understanding why we do what we do, making deep and meaningful connections, laughing, crying, sharing hugs – and so I am usually emotionally wrung out by the time I get home. The girls are ready to be all over me, and I am ready for hugs from them.

But there is something special about coming home that first night, after all the hugs and stories, when we have finally gotten the kids sent off to sleep.

When the world feels right, and all I want to do is curl up with my partner and go to sleep.

LATE PERIODS

My period is late. Only by one day – but we have been wondering for a couple weeks if we had miscalculated. No one wants to discuss birth control, or avoidance, or whatever it is that married couples do to not have babies popping out all the time. Some of us, contrary to the size of our families, do not actually enjoy being pregnant. Some of us actually really hate it.

But there was a nocturnal coupling while we were half-asleep, and I know I ovulated within 24 hours, so there is definitely a bigger chance this month than most. I've also had some constant nausea for the past few weeks and I've been feeling like my brain is not completely here. And then of course there is the fact that my ability to lift heavy objects suddenly failed me last week while moving compost (which happened just before we found out I was pregnant with my third child and we were in the process of moving). So I am overly suspicious.

The expired pregnancy test from the dollar store that I had in my house was negative last week, but it is almost a year past its expiry date, and my period wasn't late yet, so does that really count? Being the mother of four children, I am not as skinny as I once was and therefore could hide this pregnancy for a while if I was pregnant, and no one would notice anyway....

Or my period is just goofing off and playing around because my eldest is starting to cycle as well. Hers is on again, off again so far, nothing super stable, though she is due about now if last month is any indication, but those hormones playing around in the air could be causing problems.

I suppose I could also be peri-menopausal at age 38. Though this would be the first symptoms of anything like that, and about a decade earlier than the women in my family usually deal with them. So who the fuck knows?

I could spend hours on the internet trying to suss it out. I could drive a half hour and pick up another pregnancy test (let's face it, ladies, those things aren't that cheap and aren't something you want to buy when your kids are in tow, am I right?) but that is not going to happen today.

More likely I will wait and see. If there has still been no sign of Aunt Flo (or Aunt Irma or whatever your code word is) by Friday morning when I am alone and in a town with a grocery store and a pharmacy, I will probably buy one. By that point, if I am pregnant, it should show up regardless of the time of day I am peeing, right? Because that first thing in the morning pee without your coffee yet sucks, especially if you are doing something more complicated than simply peeing on a stick. Those dollar store tests require peeing in a cup and then adding exactly three drops and waiting three minutes. Waiting to see the results of a pregnancy test are some of the longest moments of your life, regardless of whether you get the outcome you want or not.

I don't even know what outcome I do want. I wasn't trying to get pregnant. But I refuse not to have quality time with the hubby whenever we can manage that around our busy life with four kids. We do our best to be safe, but nothing is foolproof except not having a sex life, and that's not an option for me.

If I am, we will deal with it. My hubby happens to love babies, so it's always a lovely surprise for him. He has never regretted my being pregnant. I actually hate pregnancy, with the morning sickness well into the second trimester and the weight gain and the constant tiredness, which is hard with other kids around. But that being said, all of my kids are now old enough to be pretty independent. I don't have any one, two, or three year olds needing to be looked after, so that would be different. I won't be climbing Mount Katahdin next summer if I am pregnant, as I'll be nursing a newborn instead, but there are worse things than that. And Mount Katahdin isn't going anywhere.

If I am pregnant, then everyone will get a refresher course on how babies are made. Perhaps my older two will be reminded about how gross birth really is, as I would plan another home birth so they would be around it again. It might keep them from having sex with boys at too young an age.

Or maybe my period is late and my body is just fucking with me? My allergies are bad, with goldenrod and ragweed everywhere. We just bought a house and moved, and had family visit, and are looking forward to having a quiet fall to catch up on rest from this crazy first half of our year. So this could all just be a trick of my body to get me to take care of myself.

Which I would totally believe, if I was just extra tired and not experiencing nausea that only goes away while I am actually eating and gets worse right after I eat. If my sense of smell wasn't heightened lately, and the place where my kids spilled sardines three days ago didn't still smell likes sardines to me even after I have washed it several times.

Time will tell. But I thought I would share this story with you anyway, regardless of the outcome, because we have all been there, right? Wondering if we are pregnant and going down the rabbit hole before we even find out if we are or not. And then having all the feelings and hormones regardless of the answer. It's part of being female.

It's part of being a mother.

But it's not something we really talk about.

Perhaps it is something we should?

WHAT ABOUT SEX?

How do you have sex around children? Because with four children, I have obviously managed it at least four times.

So here is the super-vulnerable truth about sex in my house.

The background is that the older three all know how babies are made because I was pregnant with at least one of their sisters and we read the books. *It's So Amazing* and *It's Perfectly Normal* are still well-used in my house. Just don't ask me to put my hands on them right now because someone will have squirreled them away somewhere.

Like everything else, our sex life evolves. What works this week may not work the next, but here are some of the things that have happened during our marriage with children.

We soon realized, after our first child who slept in our bed, that if we worried about enjoying each other while she was sleeping next to us, we would never get to have any fun or any kind of a sex life. Our babies were always more likely to sleep through the whole process if they were near us than if we tried to do it while they were in the other room. So we got creative and we managed it, when we weren't too sleepy, tired, or exhausted (and sometimes even when we were).

For a lot of years it happened around an infant because there was always a small person in our house until very recently. Occasionally we would get babysitters, but that was always more for having adult conversations that would not be interrupted, and I don't even mean the sexy kind, just the regular *this is what is going on in my life, what about yours?* kind of conversations.

Because my husband and I met as pen-pals, our fall-back way of communicating is still in writing. Via email (mainly for logistics) and texting and chatting, we almost always have those lines of communication open, even when we are fighting or not seeing eye-to-eye about something.

Sexting is not something we have ever really done, though we do flirt that way from time to time. Hugs when someone arrives home is always something we do, some time in that first 10 minutes or so (because there are four children who often have needs and demands as well), regardless of who was the one that left the house. We have never been shy about kissing and holding hands in front of our daughters.

I don't know what is truly regular in terms of frequency, and there have certainly been times for both of us when we didn't feel like it was happening enough (like when I was bleeding for two weeks every month thanks to a bad reaction to an IUD), and other times when we have had a comfortable middle.

Now it tends to happen mainly at night. We mostly have our bed and room to ourselves. Our eldest shares an inner wall with our room and occasionally complains about our giggling – which is usually simply us giggling and releasing the emotion of the day rather than anything more adult. But my hubby and I feel that it has only been in recent history where parents slept far away from their children (one-room log cabin, anyone?) and therefore kids have been overhearing sex lives for a long time and they have made it to adulthood just fine.

For a while my kids thought that if we were kissing in bed we must be having sex, and we have been known to start kissing to simply get them to leave the room, whether we have gone any farther than that or not. I swear we probably spend more time trying to figure out how to watch the Mature-rated TV shows than we do about figuring out how to have private time with each other.

Oh, and showers! I almost forgot about those. The kids have let us take showers together without being interrupted for a long time, so we have been known to use that for private time as well.

I guess in a way it's a bit like Santa Claus. One of these days the kids will figure out what is happening behind the scenes, magic-wise, and until then they are happy with what they can see on the surface.

It also helps that I am not really a prude. After all, I spent 11 years pregnant or nursing, so a lot of what little modesty I had went out the window. I think having a household of girls has been harder on my hubby. There have certainly been words and conversations he never expected to be part of, especially during potty training. But I am not sure boys would have been anything different.

Surely suggesting that things don't go up in there isn't much different than encouraging your son to keep his hands out of his pants? Both genders need to be reminded that touching themselves is best done in the bathroom or other private locations.

I don't know how other families do it, because I don't ask and I mainly don't want to know. That's what romance novels are for, if you enjoy them, and otherwise I am happy to let what happens in the bedroom (and other areas of the house) remain in the privacy of the people involved. I do know that my kids are calmer when my sex life is going well; there does seem to be truth to the saying "when Daddy and Mommy are happy, the kids are more secure." I am not going to say happy or calm, because lots of things affect that, but they do seem more secure with their world.

THERE IS A CAT

There is a cat
Sitting on my lap
And she's just as distracting
as a child.
She is purr-y
And fuzzy
and oh so love-y
But she is just as good
as my daughters at
keeping me from working
and as far as she is concerned
I should just be petting her
over and over and over again,
stroking her fur
scratching her head.
She pushes my fingers and hands
away from typing on the keyboard
But unlike my girls
She doesn't want to play
She simply wants to be
worshiped
Because that is her way
and the way of most
Cats.
This one seems to like me best
And all I did to deserve this
Attention
was ignore her when she first
moved in.
I let my hubby and the girls
Love all over her
While I continued with my life
and getting things
Done

And now I am her favorite one
To ask to love her.
I rarely seek her out
Other than to make sure she is
In fact in the house
Before we leave or night falls
But most of the time
It is she who comes
To find me
To lie on the floor
While I am working
To steal sips of my
Coffee
To cuddle up with me
For naps or bedtime
(Especially if it's really hot).
She doesn't seem to mind
The girls, this second-hand
Cat of ours.
She shows up when they cry
and she sleeps on their bed
She bosses them around
To make sure she's fed
She loves on my hubby
And climbs in his lap at night
For snuggles and rubs
and to crawl under his blanket
On the extra chilly nights
But she seems to follow me around the most
Hanging out
Keeping away the ghosts
And just keeping me company
Day in and day out
Which most of the time is
silent
And only needs a few pets

And isn't the demanding,
hungry
whiny
love of my girls
Instead.

I STEAL BABY SNUGGLES - I CONFESS!

I have a confession to make. I have been stealing
snuggles, from a baby that is not my own. From a cute
little boy who is under three months old but like my
babies, already weighs about 15 pounds.

He is totally not mine. He is a dear friend's
unexpected gift, that beautiful *uh-oh* that some of us
are lucky enough to receive. Mine is almost five - when
the hell did that happen? And more importantly, how
have we managed to keep her alive this long?

He's a beautiful healthy fourth child with three older
siblings who are close in age to my four and more
importantly all play together beautifully. So much so
that neither I nor their mom minds looking after the
other's kids because it ends up being less work for us,
less cranky whining and more kids outside. We joke
that we just have to throw food at them from time to
time and other than that we can ignore the collective
seven of them.

But I have been stealing snuggles from this wee one.
His parents don't mind. They are both staying at home
full time and are happy for anyone else to hold his
royal heaviness for a while. When we can visit on
weekends, my hubby also comes to snuggle this wee

one. I am reminded of that side of my husband that only comes out when holding the very small. He's got a special smile just for the babies in our lives.

Before the arrival of this community baby, I was considering one more. I'm approaching 40, so it seemed like a good time to think about if we're fully done having kids or not. But after spending a while with this one and being reminded of everything that comes with a newborn... we're done. Seriously. We're good over here!

The joy of getting to help look after this small one and getting to visit him an average of every 10 days or so is that we only get the best parts. One time I arrived on a day where he had been cluster-feeding all night and his mum was more than happy to hand him off, and the timing was such that he took a three hour nap on me. *Joy.*

He's a pretty happy baby most of the time from what I gather, but I am so very grateful he is not interrupting *my* sleep. I am also grateful not to have nursing mama brain. My dear friend complained today, when she couldn't get words out, that she does know words, she's a writer, for goodness sake!

I would happily change his diaper, and I am totally signed up for helping keeping him alive for the next few years (I always found the toddler years especially difficult to parent) especially since it will be just for visits and then he will go back home and back to his mother and family.

Especially since he comes with his other siblings that keep my kids super busy playing outside and making stuff.

Especially since right now he usually just needs someone to hold him, bounce or walk him around, and now that he is starting to smile, someone to make faces with. I intimately know the signs of hunger from a nursling and I am happy to hand him off.

Maybe this is what being a grandparent is like? Getting the snuggles and the sleepy cuddles without all the gross bodily fluids? Getting to see the light in my daughters' eyes when they get to hold him. Feeling like I am giving back for all the help I asked for and received when mine were small. I really don't mind. We are happy to help.

The reward of baby snuggles are more than worth it. I remember what a relief it was to have someone else hold my baby for a while.

Hopefully we are helping to provide breaks to this family, and it's not really just our selfish desire to hold this sweet little soul. At this time next year we will be helping keep him safe as he starts to really explore the world and get into all the things that we all must get into when we start walking around. I know how fleeting this time is. Every time I see him he is bigger. Our visits are infrequent enough that I can see the growth, but frequent enough that he recognizes me when I get to hold him, and snuggles right in.

So that's it, I confess! I am a baby snuggle stealer! And I don't plan on changing it anytime soon.

I'm Ignoring My Kids, How About You?

I am trying to write.

My youngest two daughters, on the other hand, think that it is time to sit in my office and paint their nails. Their nails, *right now,* while chattering no, make that, shouting at each other. While I am trying to write.

While I *am writing,* because I have gotten good at the art of selective hearing. It's not just for men any more.

I am not really listening to them. I am doing my utmost to ignore them.

Seriously, I am tuning out the noise as much as humanly possible and just listening for some key words or sounds. *Mom,* which can be continued to be ignored for at least an additional 30 seconds. *Accident,* now that requires instant investigation. Synonyms are *oops, darn it, did you see that* said in the right tone and *I'm sorry.*

But the general squabbling, - wait, I mean talking – that can be ignored. Completely. So I can write this for you to read, while you are probably ignoring some strange chattering sounds your kids are making.

Unless you are reading this in silence. If that is the case then you had better STOP reading. RIGHT. NOW. Because we all know that if the kids are awake and with you, sounds of silence need to be investigated. Unless of course they are teenagers. But even then, if there are any other teenagers involved, I plan to investigate. Because you never know. It may be perfectly harmless. But if it's not then I want to know what is going on.

Right now.

But as long as I can hear them, as long as they are chatting and fighting and making noise, then I can write this for you.

Is it any wonder by the time my hubby comes home at night my ears are tired? That my auditory load is overwhelmed? That if I have to listen to one more fucking word from my kids I might explode? Okay, the last bit isn't EVERY night. Just sometimes. When is playing outside *without wet icky stuff tracked inside my house* happening?

Wait, can you hear that? I can't either.

Time to find out what is going on!

It's All Phases

Watching Kids Grow

I think it is super easy to watch your kids grow in the beginning. Especially with the advent of cameras in your back pocket (aka phones) so that you can take digital photos at a moment's notice of every cute and not-so-cute thing your precious child does.

I also think that digital cameras have made the playing field more level. I don't think fewer photos get taken with the more children you have anymore. I actually think there are more photos of my younger two children as babies and in general, because by that point we had the camera in the back pocket, than of my first two. But I digress.

I think as kids get older, though, it's harder to capture them in photos. They go through that stage where they don't want to be photographed, or they always insist on sticking their tongue out in every photo (please tell me it's not just my kids who do this!). And once you hit the preteen years it's like pulling teeth to get them to allow you to take a photo, ever.

But yet your kids are still growing. They are still learning new things, and as they get older and work on getting more independent, more and more of that growing takes place away from you. At school, friends' houses, after school activities, scouts, etc. Days can start to blur together and it can be harder and harder to stop and actually see your kids for where they are right now.

You know, like when they suddenly change their favorite color or animal and totally forgot to tell you (at least when you were listening).

Or when they get really good at writing their letters, or catching a ball, or suddenly their vocabulary has gotten bigger.

It can be so easy to just let all those things slide by unnoticed. About six months ago I realized that I was getting really frustrated with my 9-year-old. She was at that point my most self reliant kid. She would just go off and do her own thing. So I would only see her when she had a problem or an issue or a complaint. I was getting really tired of all the whining, until one day I stopped to think about it and noticed that hours and hours would go by and she wouldn't come and see me because she was busy doing her own thing. I realized that I was only seeing her when she needed help with something, and that most of the time she was content with herself.

That was a powerful shift in my thinking; to understand that for her, most of the time she was happy and content, and that I was only being asked to interact with her when things weren't okay. That unlike my other kids, she didn't tend to show up to just hang out. She was too busy being off and exploring her world. I really wasn't raising a whiny upset kid, that was just all I was seeing because she solved the smaller things on her own.

That is part of what I mean by finding ways to see your kids right where they are at. In a busy house (and whether you have one kid or six, chances are your house is busy) this can be super hard to do. Especially as some of your kids get older and are less likely to catch on fire constantly so need you to be there for them. Especially if you still have younger children who are likely to catch fire and need your constant (or near-constant) attention.

So how do you see your kids? How do you absorb them where they are right now? Because let's face it, they may not pose for a photograph. I think family meals can help, whether or not they are dinner. Maybe breakfast is a better time to connect with your family. Maybe when you are driving them to or from their activities is a good time to connect. Maybe limiting how many outside activities your kids are allowed to do at any one time will help you find the time to connect.

Maybe going around the table and each saying one thing you are thankful for can help you not only change your thinking toward gratitude, but allow you be in the moment with your kids as you listen to what they find grateful about this day.

My family often likes to take walks after dinner when the sun is still up and it's not freezing outside. Or we watch how-to videos on YouTube and talk about what we are watching. Tabletop games are always a big thing that gets bigger as they get older and are less likely to throw fits when they lose and can understand more complex games.

Having one weekend day a week where we don't have social obligations is a big part of connecting as a family. Going on dates with each of your kids as often as you can is another great way to find out where they are right now and connect with them on a deeper level.

How do you keep in the moment with your kids? Because tomorrow they will be different.

SHE MOVED OUT OF MY BED

She moved out of my bed. Our youngest child moved out of our bed again. We had managed it this last fall, when she would fall asleep downstairs with me and hubby and then we would carry her upstairs where she would snuggle in with her big sister and sleep most of the night, not coming to climb back into our bed until some time in the wee hours of the morning.

But then just before Christmas, and I really think it was all that excitement and unknown about Santa Claus's impending visit, she stopped falling asleep early.

She stopped falling asleep full stop outside of my bed, curled up in the crook of my arm. Which sounds sweet, it really does, but is not that super sweet when you have a really long 4 year old who is all elbows and knees that either sleeps between you and your hubby, or just manages to shove you into the other person or out of the bed all night long.

But then lately she was talking about how she wants to sleep with her biggest sister again when we move at some yet unforeseen future date. After a couple of really bad nights sleeping with her, my hubby and I got to thinking, through a series of emails back and forth while we were both working. We figured out that we could rearrange the office (aka our third bedroom) and make it so there could be a mattress on the floor where our oldest and youngest girls (forever known as the bookends) could sleep together and then the middles could continue to sleep in their room. We could continue to keep all the clothes, and toys and general crap in the main girls' bedroom.

So on Saturday, after a long morning of Girl Scouting, I came home and started moving the two big pieces of furniture that needed to come out of the office and into our bedroom so that I can work in my bedroom in the morning and not wake up the sleeping baby (seriously she needs to get as much sleep as possible). While it's not perfect, and there is still some more sweeping and other forms of de-cluttering that need to happen in both rooms, we did make it better, and now for the last three nights my youngest has not slept in our bed.

It feels beautiful and luxurious. I am actually more sleepy right now because you know how you start catching up on your sleep debt or you start getting better sleep, and then you actually need more sleep? It's like your body realizes that you are actually giving it what it needs so it demands more of it because it thinks you've hit the mother lode.

That's where I am right now. So as much as I would love to start incorporating the 5:30 am wake ups again so that I could have some alone time to start every day, I can't do that quite yet. I really need to give myself a chance to catch a bit more sleep, and we are still getting the new bedtime routine down. But it should work out and be something I can bring in, in a week or two.

I am crossing my fingers that this is going to be a more final solution, that she is going to stay sleeping with the warm body of her sister. Because after all, most humans sleep with another person for most of their lives, and right now even though there seems to be a great age difference between 11 and 4, they are both sleeping a lot better than they were before, and the middles also seem to be catching up on sleep.

I need a slightly better curtain in that room for them. I would like them to sweep in there at least once a week so we can keep the floor tidy. A lot of the remaining de-cluttering is my husband's rather than mine, so we will see how that can start to happen.

But I am ever so grateful to have her out of my bed. Even though my hubby and I are not sleeping super close together yet because we are still luxuriating in not having knees or elbows digging into our backs and other soft places, I know that will change as our bodies can start to believe that the lots-of-limbs creature is no longer taking up most of the space in our bed.

I am looking forward to continued good night's sleep. Fingers crossed, knock on wood and no major life traumas for the next little while, please!

A Note to My 4-and-a-Half Year Old: Connecting Into Screaming

There have been a lot of very strongly-felt emotions in my house lately. When you are four, that often means a lot of screaming. Loudly. Because, when you have three other sisters, sometimes you are sure that the only way you can possibly be heard is by screaming.

Even when you haven't started at a normal volume. Because screaming gets so much better results so much faster as well. It doesn't matter if it seems rude – it just works and when you are four, getting things to work the way you want them to is the most important thing.

But it is hard for those of us who live with you, who want to communicate with you and make things better, but at the same time don't actually want to be shouted at. Especially when we are right next to you, or when you walk into the room at volume 11.

Yet I know this is partially a phase. That while it feels like you are being louder than your sisters ever were at this same age of 4, you probably are not, you are all probably about the same. It is just that with each additional daughter there has been an additional voice and that is what makes it all seem, well, just so much louder.

There are times when we have physical reactions to you, when we honestly just cringe at the sound of your voice because it is so LOUD. Because even though six months ago you were really good at using your pleases and thank you's, now you don't want to use them at all. You just want to clearly speak what you need, and right now it usually comes out as demands.

This is a hard stage for me to parent. Because on the one hand, I am so excited that you can finally most of the time tell me clearly what you need and want (as the difference between the two doesn't make sense in your brain yet). But by the same token, the way you are demanding rather than asking, the way you are yelling rather than speaking, the way you are at times just so rude, makes it really hard for me to respond in a loving manner.

I want to teach you the skills so that you will understand that you catch more flies with honey than vinegar, or in your case, shouting.

I want to teach you that you can tell the Universe clearly what you want, without losing any of your power, but also without sounding like a complete and utter bitch. I don't want you to be given those labels of bossy, arrogant, and bitchy just because you can clearly state your needs, you know what you want, and you are relentless about going after those things.

That is super powerful. At four-and-a-half you can already do that. I am so proud of you. At the same time, you absolutely exhaust me. Not because you shouldn't shine as bright as you are, but because, well, the society we live in thinks I should tame you somehow. As if I could or should dull your edges so you don't shine so bright.

I don't want to do that. However, I do know that when you can explain your needs and desires in ways that work for all the parties involved, when you can create win-win situations, when you know how to win friends and influence people, that things go easier for you. People come to bat for you, and you can make exceptions to almost any rule, and ask for forgiveness later.

These are tools I also want to give you. These are weapons as helpful as swords and arrows and a really loud voice. Being able to influence others to see your side and actually want to help you, now that is a gift that really will help you change the world to the way you want it to be.

That is what I am trying to model and teach you, oh dear 4-year-old. That you can get your sandwiches cut just the way you want and you can get all the milk you need in your bowl of oatmeal. But that by asking me nicely you will get it faster and I will feel better giving it to you. That your joy can shine through even when you ask with a smile.

Demands only get you so far – and when it comes to your three older sisters, it is really not very far at all. They don't want to play with you if you get too loud, too bossy, too demanding, too bitchy. They don't want to even be around you when you are like that, and let's face it, when they are like that you don't want to be around them either.

So how can we meet in the middle, my youngest love? How can you learn to ask nicer while not losing any of your ability to articulate to the best of your ability what it is in fact you want? I don't want to feel like you are bossing me around and telling me what to do. And you need to get your needs met.

Where is the middle ground?

Will you come and help me find it?

Can we practice balancing here together?

TEENAGE ANGST

No one told me that teenage angst starts well before they become teenagers. At least if they have two x chromosomes it does. I swear it starts at like 9.

With my firstborn, my hubby and I were on the receiving end of all the attitude and explosive emotions and all the pain as her body developed and grew. At almost 11 ½ she still hasn't become a woman in any sense of the word, but some of the emotions have settled down a little bit, at least compared to her 9-year-old sister.

My second-born has thrown most of her attitude at her sisters. She appears to be this lovely, easy-going, and generous 9-year-old that you would love to have as your buddy in Girl Scouts or on your building team. But if you are her sister, not a day goes by (and sometimes it feels more like not an hour can go by) where she is not screaming, yelling, or otherwise in a huff just because you exist.

We didn't spot it immediately because it wasn't directed at us. We didn't even realize it was happening. I am still not totally sure how much it is happening, because you know, I am not with them 24/7 and giving them my full attention, I have a business and household to run as well.

But it is happening. We can hear it in the timbre of her voice – in how quick she is to fly off the handle. It's as though something has happened since she turned 9 and her ability to hold onto her shit instead of losing it has disappeared.

Dinner time is not a lot of fun anymore. She is rude to her sisters, forgets her pleases and thank you's, and is often overly tired anyway. Combined with my 11-year-old who should be crowned the queen of sulking and holding a grudge, it can make for a very interesting table. My youngest at four is having a very hard time communicating exactly how she wants things to go and to be. Because of that she is often throwing those intractable tantrums that only a 4-year-old can throw. At least most of the time my 6-year-old is pretty mellow.

Maybe I saw these warnings before I had kids. I might have just ignored them in my pre-kid bliss brain of *I've been a camp counselor, I can handle this shit*. I think mainly I heard that it's the teenagers that are hard to deal with, that take more time than the toddlers, that are the emotional roller coasters without a prefrontal cortex to soften any of their edges.

I missed the memo about the 9-to-12 year-olds. Totally missed it. It's funny because during my years as a camp counselor, that was always the group of kids I was given. The 8-to-12 year-olds was always where I started.

But I guess because I was "public" and therefore not their parents, I didn't see them at their worst. Or maybe it was that they slept in their own tents and not in mine, and I had them at most for three weeks at a time, that made a difference. Anyone can get through 3 weeks, right?

When they are your own kid and they don't go away and no matter how hard you think about the fact that they come into the world with their own personality, it can at times be very hard to not take their behavior personally. Either as a reflection of you, or aimed at you, when often you are just their safe person to help them try and deal with the emotions that are overwhelming their body.

It is still yucky winter here, so some of the tools that help my preteens are a little harder to reach. Once it gets a little less icy we can do more hiking.

There is something about being out in the woods climbing a hill that seems to calm my kids down and helps them work out all the frustrations of being in their bodies. My eldest is often in the lead and my middles are busy chatting and my youngest is either holding my hand or her dad's and up the hill we go.

I need the weather to break just a little so we can do this. I am personally getting a little tired of walking the neighborhood, though I still try and drag them out to do it every day. For some reason this year the dance parties aren't really working. Maybe it's a lack of floor space, or maybe they just have too many opinions about how they should dance. Maybe it's because every time I think of holding a dance party all I can see is the mess they have yet to clean up on the floor. I don't know, I just know that hasn't been working very well.

We need something. We need to find new ways to communicate, to help my daughters learn to deal with their raging hormones and emotions and to understand that sometimes you just have to lean into the feeling so that you can move on to the next one. Ignoring it or trying to tamp it down only makes it blow up in your face later. Not that I have that one completely worked out myself. I am still working on feeling like it is safe enough to cry.

Maybe I could just convince them to get a little more sleep? Because sleep is an important part of all this growing and getting bigger, and when they sleep I can sleep, or at least not have to be a parent for a while. All this parenting gets so tiring sometimes. So very, very tiring.

And just think – in three more years I will have another 9-year-old, with another one about 20 months behind her. I wonder if I will have any more wisdom, or if they will have just come out of left field as well?

PUBESCENT

Pubescent
on the brink
not knowing where you are
body changing
rearranging
from one day to the next
hormones raging
who asked them?
I was doing fine before you arrived
moods shifting
like bumps on my face
Some days I am so full of hate
of all the change

all the angst
all the rearranging in my brain
thinking
sleeping
where did happy thoughts go?
Sleeping
thinking
always dreaming of life
I do not know
what I want
or who I am
or how this new story
is supposed to go
One moment up
the next down in despair
this emotional roller coaster
has got to go
when will it end
this trying on hats
When will I know
where I am at?
When will life slow down again
when can I become a caterpillar
in my chrysalis?
Can you wake me up
When it's all done?

MENARCHE FAIRIES

We have a Tooth Fairy. I think most families celebrate the putting of lost teeth that have come out of small children's mouths under pillows and then having them exchanged for coins.

In my house we started the tradition of fairy gold. For your first tooth lost you get a gold charm bracelet with the single charm of a fairy on it. Then, for each additional tooth, you leave the same charm bracelet in a small organza bag with your tooth on the dining room table downstairs and when you wake up in the morning you will find a new charm attached to your bracelet.

After three out of my four daughters have lost teeth, there has been many a tooth fairy fail and near miss. I know some of my friends who actually set alarms, but that has never worked for my husband and I. Because of these misses and near misses our Tooth Fairy has several different rules than the fairies that deliver to other people's homes.

- Our tooth fairy has until 8 am to deliver.

- Our tooth fairy needs the charm bracelet on the table downstairs because she is afraid of cats.

- Our tooth fairy is occasionally so busy that she miscalculates whose charms she needs and may need to come the following night because she didn't realize you had a loose tooth (this had to happen the first time with a nice note from the tooth fairy as my eldest lost her first tooth before she was 5 and I wasn't prepared!).

- Our tooth fairy does not deliver while camping because you might lose the charm since you won't have the bracelet.

- Our tooth fairy does not deliver on Christmas Eve because it is too confusing and too much magic is being used for Santa and the elves that night.

- Our tooth fairy did manage to deliver in New Zealand, though she brought a pair of earrings instead of a charm bracelet.

- Our tooth fairy will give you your "believe" charm when you are not sure she does actually exist, or you checked the bag before 8 am and you didn't think she had arrived.

- Our tooth fairy is really thinking that alcohol should be left out with the tooth to ensure more timely delivery of the charms, but has never actually shared this request with our daughters.

Both my husband and I have taken care of messaging the tooth fairy and trying to remember where the pliers are. We have always been good at keeping most of the charms in one location so we know where they are, but we have yet to manage to keep a set of pliers in the same place. I was specific when we moved about knowing where we put them at all times because Murphy's Law of Parenting says we would need them if I didn't know.

The girls have loved their bracelets, and how their charms often represent either something they really like or something new they have been doing lately, like sewing machines, cupcakes, and their favorite totem animal. Thank goodness for occasional grown-up-only trips to Claire's and taking earrings apart is all I am going to say.

Right now our tooth fairy is delivering to two out of four daughters, though our youngest should be coming online whenever she finally starts to wiggle her teeth. The space between her teeth in her bottom jaw is almost as much distance as another tooth right now, so I know those teeth will be ready to come out soon.

My eldest has already lost all of her baby teeth, since she started so early and has just kept going pretty consistently. Her charm bracelet was almost full before we realized that we were getting so close to the finish line. I blame the fact that she was consistently losing teeth at the same time my younger two daughters were cutting their baby teeth and I was just a wee bit distracted. She has been cleared of needing braces and now it's just a matter of finishing bringing in her 12-year-old molars and probably bringing in her wisdom teeth around 15, if she takes after her parents.

Oh and by the way, what are you supposed to do with all those teeth? At first I tried to keep them, but I soon realized that I had no idea whose tooth was whose anymore – and where do you keep them that the kids will never find them?

However, there was one thing for my eldest that I was still hiding with the tooth fairy paraphernalia – her welcome-to-becoming-a-woman kit.

Not a box of pads or tampons, though I had those on hand for her as well. No, years ago I found a lovely woman on Etsy who makes Goddess pendants out of clay and who created little menarche kits with a bracelet, some stones, a Goddess pendant, and a crescent moon pendant. The idea being that your daughter could wear the crescent moon when she is having her moon time and quietly signal what is going on without announcing it to the whole world. I thought it would be really helpful to clue her Dad in, as they are super close and he is pretty attuned to my cycle.

Which got me thinking about the need for a menarche fairy, after giving my daughter her kit this past month. I have talked to her about having a red tent party and suggesting that she might want to do it sometime in the first six months of starting. I know that she may never want to have one, as she is that child. But I feel that it is important to offer.

Should we have a menarche fairy that delivers gifts when you first bleed? I want to have the red tent party so my daughter knows she is surrounded by a community of women who love her and who she can talk to about these things and other things when she doesn't feel comfortable talking to me about it (and I know that is going to happen, it is part of the process of becoming an adult).

But I learned a long time ago never to push this daughter. My younger three will probably be super excited to have a red tent party and sit in a circle of women and be showered with attention and wisdom. But I have no idea with my eldest.

I remember being so annoyed about starting my period when it happened to me. It was inconvenient, it happened at a acquaintance's house, I thought my parents were going to be mad at me (of course they weren't), it happened a year before my mom, and in the end I celebrated by buying myself a milkshake. My eldest doesn't see why she needs to celebrate anything.

I have also crossed into the land of *it's not my place to share this information with anyone else.* I asked her if she wanted to tell her Dad or if she wanted me to (she chose the latter, so the poor man got it in a text message). I did tell her Girl Scout leader because she was going on a camping trip while she was probably still bleeding and I wanted to give them a heads up (I told my daughter that I needed to let her leader know, so I was totally transparent).

But beyond that, I haven't shared the information with anyone she knows. I did share it in my business coaching group of women, who will all keep it to themselves; we provide each other with that kind of support. But I haven't told my Mom or my best girlfriends because they are all in my daughter's life and it's really not my place to tell.

Which brings me back to the menarche fairy. Maybe it should become a thing.

Maybe it's too childish for this majorly big step in growth? She's not even 12 yet, so it's hard to know. She still plays dolls with her youngest sister from time to time.

So far she is just taking it in stride, and we are not yet on the same synced cycle. So far I am giving her more space. But she is coming to me with questions, so that is good. I have a whole section of our library filled with positive being-a-women books, including the hard to find *Her Blood is Gold*. I had purchased a book on Amazon probably less than a year ago that is in picture book format about how to take care of yourself during your first and subsequent moon times. Even though she is not a confident reader yet, she squirreled the book away after we found it while unpacking and was really glad to have found it.

We will see. Everything changes. I may be welcoming the menarche fairy along with the menopausal crone by the time my youngest gets there. This is the cycle of life, whether we like it or not.

EARLY RISERS AND NIGHT OWLS

A lot of people – and by people I am specifically talking anyone from babies to octogenarians – seem to fall into one of the two camps of early risers and night owls. Or morning people and stay-up-all-night people.

I am not sure where the middle people are. I think I am one of the middle people, because left well enough alone I get up with the sun, which is quite early in the summer and quite late in the winter, and am happy to go to bed within an hour or two of sunset. Last night I was falling asleep on the couch before the sun had gone to bed, but I think that was because I hadn't actually gotten any siesta time yesterday. I digress.

Regardless of whether you are a morning person or a night owl, you inevitably give birth to at least one child who is the opposite of you, especially if your partner is different than you are. Though I hear it can happen spontaneously, too.

My firstborn was very definitely a night owl from the moment she was born. I remember my hubby complaining about it to my mother-in-law and her just cackling on the other end of the phone, because he was finally getting his just desserts.

My eldest also wouldn't sleep all night at least once a month for her first nine months or so, but again I am digressing, back to the sleep-deprived points of my life.

So we gave up on the idea of putting small people to bed at 6 pm, because it never worked with our first daughter and that just sort of set the tone for our parenting. I suppose we could have tried to figure out what worked for each subsequent child, but the pattern was already set and they just kind of evolved into it.

Whoever is the baby doesn't get sent up to bed around 8 or 8:30 pm, but everyone else does. At this point no one is the baby, so they all get sent up to bed. It takes them at least half an hour to sort themselves out and settle down, and my hubby and I take a hands–off approach and try and get some TV watching in for a few minutes before going to bed ourselves.

This has worked reasonably well for years. Lately my eldest, whose biological clock is deep into puberty, has been needing to stay up later at night. There is neuroscience behind this need and they have discovered that melatonin release is a good two hours later in teenagers than it is in adult brains, so it's not surprising that she may need to stay up later.

I am not a night owl. However, from about the time I was 11 or so until shortly after my 18th birthday, I was. Since I was homeschooled, I would literally be doing my math or Latin or physics at 1 or 2 in the morning and then go to bed around 3. I would then sleep until noon and then get up again. My parents were pretty accommodating and I got a lot of alone time, which I needed during that period of development. There also wasn't social media back then, and not much beyond email, so I couldn't get into a lot of trouble. I didn't have a computer or a TV in my room so I was left with a radio, which had to be kept low, and my books. It worked for me.

The upside of my kids homeschooling and going to bed a little while later than maybe other people's kids

(I was going to use the word average, but I actually don't think any of us really know what average is in this department) is that I get at least an hour in the morning (depending entirely on how soon I drag myself out of bed), and sometimes two or three, alone. Which is the only way I stay sane some days.

If it is an overcast or rainy morning I get even more alone time, as their rooms stay darker longer, regardless of any blackout curtains they may or may not have.

My hubby is still a night owl. But he has learned to get up early in the morning and go to work so that he can get his work done and have more of his "best" time at home with the family. It is possible that as more of the girls move into more of a night owl routine themselves that he may adjust his work schedule slightly so he can stay up with them more at night and have more bonding time. We will just have to wait and see.

In the meantime, I try and let my girls keep their own hours for waking and sleeping, generally trying to insist they be in their rooms after dark until it gets light again. There is always much grumbling about having to get up early in the morning on the rare (usually less than once a week) occasions that happens. At some point I think we will set up a cozy corner in our sunroom for children who are having trouble sleeping or have later biological clocks than the rest of us. Short of setting up a room in the basement, that's the best I am going to be able to do right now.

Do your kids keep the same sleep schedule as you do? I think that might actually drive me crazy if they did, as I get the most tired when my kids get up with me and go to bed with me and I have no time to myself that is predictable and I know is coming.

FRONTAL LOBES

They are arguing in the next room. I can hear them squabbling over nothing very important, just establishing the pecking order that even girls need to have. It may not be as straightforward as male pecking orders - the hierarchy may change more often and be far more subtle - but it still happens. You can't put four girls - and in the blink of an eye they will all be young women - in a house together and not have fights, disagreements, and just plain upsets.

It gets tiring when they are little, though. They resort to physical violence to defend themselves if they are too young to get the words out. Then you have to deal with the fact that they didn't get the words out and they probably should have and it just becomes a thing. Grown-ups have to get involved and that never feels really great. Nope, that ends up feeling really icky after a while, having to have grown-ups involved in squabbles and fights that seem nonsensical to grown-up brains.

Because here's the thing: those lovely children of ours, and teenagers too, scarily anyone under the age of 25 to 30, are not actually functioning with a full brain yet. That most important part, I would say probably one of the key reasons we are human and not like the other animals, that frontal lobe, is the last part of the brain to come in. Research now shows that it often doesn't come in until we are 25 to 30 depending on gender and life experiences, and let's face it, we all have our own biological clocks that tick at their own rates.

Which means most of us will have gotten married to the person we plan to spend the rest of our lives with and probably have had our first babes all before our brains are fully developed. No wonder we sometimes outgrow our partners later. Just when your brain is fully coming on line, you are now facing sleepless nights and the needs of small people, which we all know can be exhausting even to the best of us, and very few of us are pretending to be the best.

What the hell? I mean, it takes so long to get that full-blown brain in. The concept that we just have to get our kids to age 18 is ridiculous, because there is so much brain development that still needs to happen even after that, for another 12 years! It's like we are only going to help out with the first 3/5ths of their brain development, and then after that they are on their own. That frontal lobe has so much to do with control and work ethics and the ability to think things through, and we are relying on social media to teach this to our kids, and excuse me while I go puke a little in the corner.

What a recipe for disaster! No wonder so many kids are suffering from anxiety. No wonder there are so many abusive relationships going on. Not to mention the effects that alcohol and drugs and tobacco have on those still very much developing minds.

It's all pretty scary. Yet here I sit, writing this while letting my girls figure their shit out. Already the sounds of their voices have moved on from that of fighting and disagreements to talking nicely and playing with each other again. I think there is some kind of imaginary game going on. The room has also gone from three girls down to two, and that always seems to help. Four or two always seems to get along better than three. I guess that is why I ended up with four?

It feels like a lifetime's work, getting our children to the point where they have their whole brains. We may be welcoming grandchildren into our arms before they get there. It is possible we will have passed on before they have all gotten there, and we can only hope that siblings and other family members will help.

It is a lot longer than we think when we hold our newborns in our arms. We are focused on their ears and little toes and feeding and changing and loving on them. We're just starting to communicate with them outside of the womb. Perhaps it is best we don't know what we are getting into, or how long we are signing up for taking care of them.

Perhaps that is best.

IN THE BLINK OF AN EYE

Years go by
In the blink of an eye.
We don't always notice
the little things that change
because we are too busy cleaning up the
muck
and gross bodily fluids of being a
grown-up

caring for these small little people
so they too can become a
grown-up
and clean up the muck of the
messes we make in our lives.
Starting with birth
and then just going from there
We all have to wipe our own
butts
at least once a day.
Life is messy
and tiring.
But we all know that being
exhausted at the end of the day
is often a recipe for sleep
And sleep is a good thing,
that surrendering
to the unknown
the letting go
of everything
and just being in a state of not-being.
Often as parents
the only time we can fully relax
and breathe a sigh
is when our kids have abandoned
themselves to sleep.
From sleeping babies
To snoring teenagers
we can often begin to rest easy
to unwind
to congratulate ourselves
On keeping everyone alive
Truly alive
for another day,
another day to grow and play
Another day to just be

But in those minutes
where we play and pick up and clean up
we sometimes miss the changes,
the length of the limbs as they grow out
How the brain upgrades
usually while we are asleep
and now this person that we have
known their whole lives
Is someone else entirely
And they didn't ask us,
we didn't give our permission,
it just happened in what felt like
a blink of an eye
and soon we will be holding
the next generation in our arms
in our hearts
and facing our own
mortality and the
legacies we hope
we are leaving behind,
and it all happens in the
blink of an eye
and the small moments
of mess cleaning up.

SEASONS CHANGE

Seasons change whether we want them to or not, and so do our kids. Sometimes it seems like the difficult stage they are in lasts for millennia because once they morph into an easier stage we don't tend to notice it has even happened. We are too busy either dealing with another kid in a similar difficult stage, or the ease of this new stage is just enjoyed without our really noticing it and then the next thing we know, we are back there again, back to another slightly newer difficult stage.

Most of these difficult stages are actually transition phases between one part of development and the next. What is funny (not really) is that this continues into our adulthood, but can at times be harder to see.

My business coach has to keep reminding me that moving to a new house is like having a baby. It takes time after you have moved in to really get your roots down. I keep thinking I should know this because this is not my first move. This is my fourth move in Maine and I have moved many, many times before. Yet each time it brings up new things, even if you are moving the same stuff. Even if you have moved before, moved with the same family before, it always brings up stuff, well after the move. Even if you think you are done processing, the rest of your family may not be.

So these difficult stages keep happening to us, even as adults. Sometimes they seem random and unfair, like the death of a loved one, the loss of a job, the need to start a new job in a new city. It is like the stages of grief; you never really know when they are going to hit you again, even though you feel like you've gone through it before.

But some stages are a bit more predictable. The birth of a new baby, getting married, getting divorced – these are obvious periods of transition and growth.

Less obvious ones include the time after those things, the periods after you have the big date, the big vacation you have waited forever for, when you are making a career change, starting a new major change in your lifestyle, getting a new pet or losing one. These are all periods of transition that we tend to ignore or not realize they have as much of an impact as they do.

Perhaps that is where the 20/20 hindsight comes from?

Autumn has arrived here in Maine. Today it is not getting above 50 degrees and it is still September. However, in two more days it will be 70 again – a classic New England fall transition.

Because of this and having just moved, and getting ready to publish this book, and do a lot of visibility and community growth as part of preparing for the launch of this book, I feel like I am in one of those icky transition periods.

My body feels different to me, and I am fighting the need to exercise and sleep and rest with equal measure. My emotions are a bit all over the show and I am finding it easy to snap at people (though most of it is staying in my head and not coming out of my mouth).

Then there is the inevitable need to prepare for winter, to work on our property and prepare for upcoming snowfall that will happen all too soon. To build a shed to be able to store the tools over the winter. To actually want to be outside exploring and enjoying the fall weather before we have to bundle up our bodies to stay warm.

There is also the drawing in. Most of my Christmas shopping is done except for the Santa-requested gifts. There are knit-alongs and quilt-alongs I want to take part of as we spend more time inside and less time outside. There is the need to gather food and supplies and books in case we get snowed in, even though we probably will not. There is the biological drive to do these things at this time of year.

All this while feeling icky. While upholding new boundaries around my work. While becoming more visible in my business.

Transition periods suck. I don't think they get any less sucky the older we get. I think we begin to learn that this is part of the rhythm of life, the ebb and flow, but I don't think it gets any easier to go through because each time it is different. Each time it is less fun – but necessary. It will happen and if you fight against it, it will just take longer. Like a toddler's tantrum or a preteen waiting for everyone to leave before she decides to talk to you.

I just want to get more sleep, or knit and sew and just have the world leave me alone. But that's not what is happening quite yet. I try to carve out time each day for those things to happen. But Monday mornings can be hard as my kids transition back into not interrupting me every five minutes in the morning.

DON'T JUDGE ME

Have you ever gone to a playdate with a group of women, maybe a moms meetup or some other social event that is supposed to be around moms and their kids, often their young kids? Have you ever shown up and then felt like it turned into a judgement fest?

I remember a mom who had to sanitize her kids' hands every time they came back to the blanket after playing on the playground. Every single time, and kids come back a lot to touch base with their mom when they are under the age of five.

I remember the time all the moms were feeding their kids fancy organic snacks in pouches. I couldn't afford fancy plastic pouch food, so I just had organic carrots and homemade hummus for them. To this day my homemade hummus, which my kids like just as well as the kind you buy in the tubs, will often be the last thing still left at a potluck. Not because it isn't yummy, but because no matter what kind of container I put it in, it is like no one can recognize it if it isn't in one of those plastic tubs you buy them in at the store. If the lids to the containers did not suck so royally, I would just wash and keep one and put my homemade hummus in it so everyone would actually think it was the store-bought kind.

I have been to beach and lake playdates where everyone shares snacks, and no matter what I bring my kids are always going to want to eat the snack someone else's mother has brought. ALWAYS. We could have both brought grapes and they are totally going to want to eat from the other side. Because while I try to bring a combination of not very expensive and still healthy food – like pretzels and hummus and a veggie and maybe a fruit – other people bring the SmartFood, oreos, and chips. Which is always more exciting.

At parties I don't mind as much. You know, the potluck ones where everyone brings something. For years I made a soba noodle salad because one of my friends absolutely loved it and it was super easy to make. I made it so much, that if I am honest I would be happy to never eat it again. These days the decision about whether I bring something I make or something store-bought is often based on how much time I have left. If we have a super busy week I will be the mother who brings the watermelon to the kids' birthday party, because you can never have too much watermelon, even if someone else brings one too.

I try to avoid conversations about eating. Someone is always on a diet. My hubby is allergic to dairy, so if he is with me I often try and find out who made what so I can see if it has any dairy in it. Because as much as I love him, he will so rarely ask for himself and then gets so grumpy when he can't get enough to eat that I just end up asking for him these days.

But seriously, it can be difficult to know what to bring. Obviously, if it's a family party, I will bring something that is dairy-free for my hubby, but then you have everyone worried about gluten, or who knows what else they aren't eating this week. It can get frustrating. As someone who grew up with people who have had serious life-threatening allergies, watching someone cheat on their gluten gets old fast.

I often think that with allergies and people choosing not to eat certain kinds of food that bringing store-bought food still in the package is the default way to go because someone can just read the ingredient list and decide for themselves if they want to consume that food or not.

Don't get me started on the drinks! I don't buy juice, soda, energy drinks, or any of that stuff. When I buy coffee out it is just with cream and no sugar. My kids are not used to sugary drinks, though if you put lemonade in front of them they will drink it happily – as much of it as they can get their hands on.

Lately they have discovered the flavored seltzer water that a bunch of my friends enjoy drinking. A lot of people think it is better than soda. I am not sold on the idea, but it is the non-alcoholic beverage of choice I will be buying for the next party we host. Because I am not providing soda, and constantly making lemonade gets old fast.

There will be plenty of water, cups with a pen to write your name on, and paper goods that we can then burn in the grill later. That's the best I can do this time. Sometimes parties are small enough to do it on reusable dishes, but honestly washing dishes for hours after a party isn't my idea of a great time. I am sure burning the plates and cups isn't good either, but that's the choice we are making this time.

Recently, however, I try not to feel judged on the food I bring to either feed my kids or to share at a potluck. Because these days there are very few foods that someone can't find an objection to. So you might as well go with something your family likes to eat and that fits in the budget you wanted to spend. That seems like the only good solution.

Coffee-Drinking Children

When my first child was born we lived in South Florida, a place full of people and hot weather and not a lot of outdoor places that weren't the beach. As a redhead with light skin, this was not a great place for me to be. I burn easily, so spending hours at the beach wasn't a good idea for me at all.

Our firstborn actually hated sand, which we used to our advantage a couple of times. When she had us up all night as a young one, we would give up and drive out to the beach to see the sun rise over the water. Once we discovered she hated sand, we would put her on a blanket or towel and then move about three feet away and have a few minutes of personal space. My hubby and I were usually completely wrung out by a night without sleep, and facing a day ahead that we needed to be awake for. The fact that she would stay on the blanket and not move off of it because she hated sand felt like a small reward for making it through the night.

The other thing we did was to go the mall to walk. We really didn't go to the mall to shop, but to just get out of the house (for a short time we lived in an apartment, and for a longer chunk of time we were back in the house with my parents and brother, so time away as just us was crucial). The only place to go and walk was the malls, or Ikea after one opened near us, though it was a lot farther away and through more traffic than the malls.

Anyway, my older two daughters grew up walking around malls or being pushed in their stroller or carried on one of our backs in a baby carrier. About the only purchase we were guaranteed to make was stopping at Starbucks for a coffee.

This was the late 2000s and my husband had a dairy allergy. One of only a few coffee shops that offered non-dairy lattes was Starbucks, and the malls did not necessarily have any other coffee shops available. If you wanted a Cuban coffee, which is an ultra sweet espresso, you could get one of those in the food court, but if you wanted a nice big cup of coffee you could walk around with, then you had to go to Starbucks. There was not another option.

My hubby would usually finish his coffee before I had finished mine, which is pretty typical, or we would be sharing a venti, which was the largest they came in back in those days, and once the cup was done, it would get passed down to our eldest in the stroller. Why? Because she loved eating up the rest of the soy foam from the latte. She thought it was yummy, so it became her special treat and it meant we got to avoid buying her anything at the coffee shop. Because let's face it, everything is overpriced in a mall, especially the food and drink.

We used to get the strangest looks from the old ladies as here was our small person (under the age of

3) drinking from a Starbucks cup. It would happen at the Barnes and Noble, too, as that was the other place we would frequent in those days. Their Saturday morning story time worked better in our schedule than the library's, and well, it was a bookstore, so what wasn't there to like? Plus they almost always had a Starbucks, so it was perfect, right?

Now, at age 12, our daughter has been periodically having her own cup of coffee for a couple of years. It's not something we buy for her, usually – though all bets are off while traveling internationally. If you want a cup of coffee on the long journey to New Zealand and back, you can have a cup of coffee. But at home, she is welcome to have some from the French press we have going. Just this past weekend she asked if she could have what was left in the French press after her Dad and I got our cups. I said yes, and noticed later that she only drank about a third of it. Which is cool.

She has always liked the taste of coffee, even if she doesn't choose to drink much of it. She will pick coffee-flavored ice cream quite happily when her choices are limited (aka we are not at the 30-flavor gelato shop – and even then she got espresso chip as one of her choices on her birthday). I only like really good coffee-flavored ice cream.

Coffee has not stunted her growth. She is already 5' 2 ½" at age 12, so there are no problems there. I really don't think the small amounts of coffee she might have gotten in the foam caused any issues when she was little. The soy milk probably had more of an impact, but we had no idea about that back then. Now she is getting pretty tall and she's beautiful and she occasionally wants a cup of coffee. I am good with that.

She never gets to put sugar in it, just milk or cream or coconut milk, so it's all good.

Nowadays the cup of foam gets passed to our youngest for her to clean out. No one else seems that interested in it (though my eldest will clean it out if no one else wants it). We don't buy coffee out that much anymore. We tend to make it at home. Our favorite coffee shop is a half an hour from our house and not a Starbucks but a locally-owned shop that carries about six different kinds of artificial milks and several dairy milks as well, and non-dairy sweets. Our waistlines only let us visit about once a month or so.

But I remember the dirty looks we used to get when our eldest, who was at the time our youngest, was playing with those Starbucks cups. Yet these same people would complain that they couldn't tell she was a girl because her ears weren't pierced (we didn't see the point in mentioning she had decided to dress all in pink and purple that day). The preconceived notions people have about kids - it's enough to drive you insane!

BABY SHOWERS

Baby showers are a time of celebration. When it's your first baby, it is also time to start getting all the things you will need after the baby is born, though you probably don't need nearly as much stuff as the baby registries and magazines would have you believe.

At the end of the day you need a carseat. A place for the baby to sleep if it's not with you. Some clothes -

and I highly recommend some kind of strap-on baby carrier, be it a wrap, pouch, sling, or our family's personal favorite, an Ergo. Some receiving blankets are also nice, but towels will work. Hand towels can double up as burp cloths as well. Most babies don't need bibs until they are several months old (and some of my daughters refused to wear them so...).

I have had three baby showers. One for my firstborn, and one each for my third and fourth born. I got a lovely card with money in it for my second born from the women I worked with and that was really helpful.

This weekend I attended a baby shower for an unexpected fourth baby. One of the things the shower host wanted us to do was to talk about the mum and the new baby, as several of us had four or more children. This family is Catholic and so were many of the attendees, so many of the comments had to do with how great a mum she is, how wonderful it was that she chose life, and how much God must have wanted her to have another baby.

I spoke about how grateful I was that we were moving closer so that we could help out as much as she would like, by either helping with the baby or just taking her older kids away so she and the baby could rest. How much my hubby and I were looking forward to holding a new baby boy as we had enjoyed holding her last one.

I was struck by how much saying *God chose for you to have another baby* really doesn't help in the middle of the night when you are so tired and the baby is not sleeping. Or in my experience, in the middle of the day after a long night when your older children want and need you and you literally have nothing left to give.

I remember the looks of contempt my eldest gave me when my all just wasn't quite good enough because of how much the baby needed. In my experience it is the toddler years that are much harder for me than the newborn months. Once the baby gets mobile (which has been faster and faster with each of my girls), my life feels over until they get to be about three. Over the past 6 months I have really struggled with how much energy being four takes, probably because I have two preteens on top of the 4-year-old.

I know that this woman is going to be held in the community, because we are lucky enough to have a community that does that. One of us will set up the "bring them a meal" website after the baby is born and a bunch of us will check in regularly. We'll offer any help we can, from washing dishes and laundry, to taking husbands and children away for a while, to holding the baby.

But this is not the case so many times. So many times women do not have a collective of other women to keep an eye on them. To help them understand that: postpartum depression can come at any point, even months after the baby is born; sometimes the first few months are easy and sometimes they are the worst marathon; some babies integrate into the outside-the-womb world well and others take a while and have a lot of crying to do.

Women don't always know that our collective community of women needs playdates at the beach, even when all our children are teenagers, or that we need girls' nights out even when the babies come, and that sometimes we just need a shoulder to cry on.

I didn't have any of this with my first two. I had my mother, father, and brother, who helped out as much as they could. But I didn't have a community of women. With our firstborn, we tried going to all the attachment parenting and LLL meetings hosted at our birth center, but we didn't really meet a lot of aligned parents there that lived close enough nearby to be friends. Plus I was soon to move from part-time to full-time work, and most of those moms were able to stay at home, which is a different experience.

It shouldn't create tension, but it often does – that difference between the mothers who have to go back to work and the mothers who stay home. Especially here in the United States, where we do not have any guaranteed time off after our baby is born, paid or unpaid. That lack of bonding time can be critical to our ability to feel like a competent mother (at least some of the time) later on.

I think baby showers should be rethought. Instead of being about getting all the baby gear you think you need, it should be about how the people who love you and this new baby can help in the first year or more of life. These can be simple things like making meals, watching the other children, or checking in via email or social media to see how the mom is doing. Things like coming to clean the house or do the dishes (or paying for someone else to come and do those things if they are not your cup of tea). Instead of tricking out the expensive crib, we could be buying some of those mail order boxed meal kits to help ease the load of even deciding what to make for dinner the next night.

We could promise to come in and hold the baby so mom can shower, or take her out for coffee or tea, or just hang out and keep her company, not just in the first few months but throughout the first couple of years. We could take on our collective *it takes a village* godparent status and really help each other out.

Now that would be an amazing baby shower.

THAT TIME SHE LICKED SAWDUST

That sounds like the beginning of a mother-of-the-bride-type speech, right? Like *I am so grateful my daughter found this special person and we are spending this special day showering her and her intended with love, but did you know that one time she ate sawdust?*

Or maybe I should keep this story until she is pregnant with her first child and is beyond the point where she can do anything but have this baby. Like during the early stages of labor?

Or when she is a teenager, to illustrate why she should not to have kids anytime soon, as well as being a cautionary tale about what could happen when she babysits?

Or maybe I just wait and one of her sisters will tell her first. Maybe she has already heard me mention it to other moms – that one time when she totally ate sawdust. What is the grossest thing your kid has ever done? Because you know we moms bond over stories like this, right? We do – when it's not an unspoken competition.

Perhaps it should just stay in the family, like a family secret or something. Like *here is a little something about my daughter.*

But here is what happened. My daughter was under the age of three, maybe two – I am a bit fuzzy on those types of details. I do remember what house we were in and I do remember that it was winter and my Mom was visiting. I am pretty sure my youngest had been born and was in arms still, or was about to be born.

Anyway, my Mom and I had gone to the grocery store with all of the kids. So my husband, in his infinite wisdom, decided to get the sawing he needed to do for whatever project he was currently working on done while we were out of the house. But he did it inside the house, because it was fucking cold outside and we didn't have any kind of sheltered place outside for him to do this work. It probably wasn't something big, it was probably just a few cuts; I really don't remember those details.

But what I do remember is coming in with my arms loaded down with grocery bags, with my mother and my older daughters all carrying stuff. Of course, here comes my toddler, not carrying anything. What does she do upon seeing that her father has left a pile of sawdust on the floor because he didn't know that this was the moment we were all going to walk in the door?

Well, you already know, right, because you read the start of this story? She got down on all fours and started licking the sawdust straight off the floor. Before anyone even knew what was happening. Before the three adults in the house could even shift gears, my little one is licking the sawdust off the floor.

She was not an overly orally-fixated child. Not every blessed thing went into her mouth, unlike some of my other children, so we weren't prepared, and we certainly weren't forewarned. She did not announce the fact ahead of time that to fully appreciate and understand the house that had changed slightly since she had just been there earlier in the day, she needed to lick it.

Nope, there was no warning. There was nothing. Just a toddler on the floor licking up the sawdust while we adults picked our collective jaws off the floor before picking her up and telling her that sawdust does not in fact taste good, is not good for our tummies, and would someone get the goddamn broom and sweep it up before we put her on the ground again?

Because at that moment we are wondering: whose child this is? How did this happen? How did we get this spawn that thinks, that even dreams, that tasting sawdust is something to do? I mean, she had some capacity to talk already. She was old enough and mellow enough that we were not expecting this.

It's not like something proud that you want to brag about. It's not like my kid made honor roll or joined Mensa. No – she licked sawdust off of the floor. Why? I am guessing because it was there.

Other than removing her from the situation and recommending that perhaps she shouldn't sample it in the future, I didn't make a big deal of it to her. I mean, life is about experiencing and trying things right? I myself was the child that had to sample the milk bones at a much older age to see why the dog liked them so much.

So in a way, I get it. I just am not sure if I have an obligation to warn any future mates of hers that this could be in the gene pool – I still think it might be helpful to discourage having children before she is fully ready (not that any of us really are, we just think we might be).

What about you? Are there any sawdust-eaters out there as well? Or is truly just this one child of mine?

WAITING IN LINES

It's that time of year when the stores and public spaces get even more crowded than normal, and we spend so much more time waiting in lines. Waiting to check out at the ever-crowded stores, waiting to see Santa, waiting to give a friend a hug at a crowded party.

As much planning as I do, and as much early buying and mail order I do, I still end up at the very least needing to go grocery shopping at least once a week during the mad rush from Thanksgiving to New Years.

Added to my pile is the fact that I live in Maine and sometimes the weather can cause extra issues with that whole shopping thing. As well as the fact that I have a deep need to pack lots of food into our house this time of year in case we get stuck for a while buried in snow.

But while we are doing all this line-waiting there is the inevitable boredom, not just from us, but any of our children we happen to have with us.

If this was a social media post I would ask you to like it, or raise your hand, if you have ever waited in line to see Santa only to have said child decide at the last minute they are really too afraid to see Santa after all.

Then there is the judgement. It is so hard to stand in line and not get bored and then start looking around and seeing what everyone else is doing and silently making up stories about what they are doing.

Who hasn't been given a dirty look by someone without children when your child starts displaying their upset about waiting?

I do my best to never give a dirty look to another mother with an upset child in public. She's got enough to deal with, without my adding to it. I have always done this, even before I had kids. But there are times, now that I have kids, that when I am getting away from them the last thing I want to do is go be where someone else's kid is upset. So I do understand the feeling that some of those dirty looks emanate from.

I am going to share a truth that we don't like to talk about, especially if you are a feminist. That truth is that those who do not have kids (and it doesn't matter whether they are your biological children or not) at a deep level do not understand what it is like to have kids. Your brain, heart, soul, and often very biology changes when you become a caretaker of someone small. It becomes so easy, and at times feels imperative, to not put on your oxygen mask first. It becomes hardwired into who you are.

I was talking to another mom a while ago about what it is like at her new job, where her boss doesn't have kids and the person in her position previously also didn't have kids. She struggled with trying to explain how the pay for her job really wasn't enough for anyone with a family. You can read all the statistics you want about how much it takes to raise a kid, but until you have it impact your money, it is just a foreign concept.

I love my friends who don't have kids. But in certain of them there is an underlying resentment that my life, while not always revolving around my kids, is certainly impacted by my kids. My schedule definitely is, even though we have limits on how many activities we take the kids to or let them be involved in.

Some of my childless friends are incredible and become much-beloved aunts and uncles to my kids and have the energy levels that only someone who doesn't have their sleep stolen by these cute beings can have. They have saved my day many a time.

So remember, when you are out in public and you feel like you are being judged by someone else about your children, regardless of what that person is actually thinking, it is only your reaction that really matters. If you feel the need to send a dirty look back, go for it. If you want to ask them to give you a hand, feel free. If you want to choose kindness over honesty and just grin and bear it, I've got your back on that one too.

We need to give each other more grace and realize that we all get hangry. Maybe waiting in line shows us at our worst, including the kid crying in the cart next to you.

GOOD PARENTING = KID SLEEPS THROUGH THE NIGHT

Why is there this myth in parenting that you are only doing a good job if your kid sleeps through the night?

It starts out with your infant. That is one of the first questions anyone asks you: is the baby is sleeping through the night yet or not? In some ways and for some people it may be a way to try and help and connect. Just about every parent has had a sleepless night or two (or years) when their children are little and having extra support, compassion, and help is wonderful.

But a lot of times that question about whether your child is sleeping through the night or not becomes one of judgement. And stress and angst. No one wants to be sleep deprived, not really. Even college students who stay up late partying and then go to work and school the next day do eventually crash, and often for days on end (or they find new stimulants to keep going and make the crash even bigger).

But infants aren't meant to sleep for hours a time. They didn't in utero and they don't once they leave the warm womb. Each infant has a different adjustment to the great big world outside their mother's body and they choose to express that in so many different ways.

I was incredibly lucky. My first two daughters would sleep for four or five hour stretches from birth. But that being said, my eldest would keep us up all night long at least once a month, often coinciding with a month since she was born, for months on end. We would end up at a 24-hour IHOP and then see the sunrise on the beach. It was so painful.

My third daughter woke me up every two hours from the get-go. It was so incredibly hard. I remember about a week after she was born crying at four in the morning, after having just seen 2 am, because I was so tired. I knew that I "shouldn't" complain because many mothers would have already been doing this from the beginning with all of their children, but that only made me cry harder. I was so fucking tired.

Some children come into this world as night owls. My firstborn is like that and now, at almost 12, she is struggling with the fact that her hormones have changed and that melatonin is being released two hours later than mine and hubby's and she is still awake and functional at 9 pm while everyone else is winding down to bed. We have explained what is going on and tried to support her by giving her space to do quiet things while she is still awake, but she doesn't like the alone time, coming to bed after her sisters are all asleep. More often than not I wake up in the morning to find her sleeping on the floor at the end of our bed.

Like the bedwetting that can happen for years after all other forms of potty training are complete, having children up at night happens a lot more than we usually share. Sometimes we admit that we were up late because a child was having a "bad dream," or we just say we didn't sleep well that night.

But like everything there can be points in our lives (often when big changes are going on, whether they affect the whole family or are just developmental leaps for your child) where there is more waking up at night than others.

Last summer my whole family lost sleep for weeks on end because of construction on the U.S. highway about 500 feet from our house. The construction workers were trying to make traffic flow better during the day, so they would move all their large metal pieces (and then drop them what felt like randomly) in the middle of the night. At times they also worked overnight with their trucks and bright lights. It got so bad and happened for so many weeks that my kids still hear construction sounds and have almost a PTSD-type reaction where they visibly cringe and get extremely anxious. We have lived in this house for almost four summers and every year there has been some type of construction going on. My kids dread seeing the orange construction signs around our house.

But why don't we share when our older kids aren't sleeping? Or when we as women are not sleeping as much due to hormones, be it pregnancy or peri-menopause related or just stress or Goddess knows why we routinely wake up between 3 and 4:30 am?

Maybe because it's the only chance we have in the day to think straight.

Maybe we have gotten so used to sleep deprivation and caffeine that we don't remember what normal sleep habits are like.

Maybe we should start finding cushy ways to sleep in the car while our kids are an activity or sport.

Maybe humans have always woken up at night until very recent history because predators are around (and some of us still don't live in safe neighborhoods).

Wouldn't it be wonderful if we had a sign? Like a pin, or badge, or thing on our purse that meant we were sleep deprived – and we could see someone else with that sign and say things like:

"Mama, you got this."

"I've been there."

"Can I help you grab a 20-minute nap?"

Wouldn't that right there make the world a better place?

FAMILY SIZE

Why do we judge people based on the size of their family? We do. All the time. I find myself not understanding families that chose not to have kids. It's not that I don't respect their right not to have children – I do, but because my experience is different there comes a point where I don't understand adult women who have never had a child.

And to be brutally honest and vulnerable, I don't know what it is like to only have one child. I grew up as one of two and I was never going to have an only child. That is why my first two daughters are exactly 1 year and 50 weeks apart, because my hubby had hurt his back and not everything was working the way it should and there was no way I was going to have only one kid, so no precautions were being taken. Nope, none at all.

But once you get past two kids, it does seem like some judgement moves in. I remember when I found out I was pregnant with our fourth child and several of my friends with four or more kids welcomed me to the large family club. Apparently having four is when you cross over to being considered a large family these days. I guess three is just borderline?

I find this all really interesting because in the 1950s it seemed like everyone had three or four children. It was the Baby Boom after all and all the literature and television from those days shows three or four children and station wagons. Like that was normal. Especially if you had two of each gender.

Growing up and playing imaginary games (because the writer in me still needed to get out) I always assumed I would have four kids, two girls and two boys. The universe is having a great laugh at me by giving me four wonderful girls.

I have friends with six, seven, and more kids and I don't judge them. As long as everyone is being fed, looked after, and loved I really don't care about the size of the family. Yes, I do think about how many kids are coming to play when I figure out snacks, and I do my best never to send my kids anywhere without food because there are four of them and they eat a lot. But that is about the extent of it. Really, having eight kids in my house at once is usually easier on me than just my four as they are all busy playing.

But I know friends of mine have felt really judged when their whole family is out in public. I have rarely experienced that. I usually get "All they all yours?" to which I reply yes. That is followed up by "Are they all girls?" to which I also reply yes. Then there is usually a comment along the lines of "Your poor husband" and something about "They are so beautiful" and that's the end of the conversation.

I don't feel bad for my husband. He was involved in the making of all of those girls, and probably had a big hand in them being girls (the science keeps going back and forth on who picks the gender, the sperm or the egg). He loves his daughters and wouldn't have it any other way. So don't feel sorry for him.

I guess because by and large my daughters are well behaved in public (because I do what I can to set it up so they can be, making sure they are fed and well rested when at all possible) that leads to the cute comments. My girls are beautiful in my eyes, but they are also smart, brave, problem solvers, and at times mischievous little shits.

I have never had anyone comment that my family is too big. Maybe, like not having people make comments about me breastfeeding in public, I am too intimidating–looking or just don't expect to have the experience so those people stay away. I don't know. But it has yet to be my experience. Yet in a lot of ways, my family is too large for a lot of things. We rarely qualify under the family rate because it is usually for two adults and two (or occasionally three) children and we have four. There are certain things we don't currently do, because for your family it might be a $50 outing and for mine it would be more like $100, and as a family we choose to spend our money differently.

I do still take my family to the movie theater from time to time for really special movies. We all went to see *A Wrinkle In Time*, and I am sure we will grab something this summer on a hot day when we need a break.

Instead of staying in hotel rooms, we are more likely to pack a tent and stay at a campground because cooking over a fire and campground fees are always less than a hotel and restaurant fees.

I even look at tabletop games differently, knowing that someday all six of us will be able to play. I am more likely to grab a game that goes up to at least six players than ones that only do four, because I dream of playing with my teenagers and young adults in the upcoming years. I spent so many happy hours doing that as a teenager and with my hubby before we had kids. We still try to grab a game as often as we can.

But why do we judge each other on the size of our families? I don't really know what it is like to have six kids, because I only have four. But I do remember what it was like to have only one, only two, and for a brief period only three. I have had four kids for almost five years at this point, so it has become my reality. It's just what I do. I have been counting my kids since we only had two (because for me that was the hardest switch, going from one child to two). Adding additional members of the family has not been as hard for me as that first switch from one to two. What is strange is that as they get older they are not always with me at all times, so having less than four is lovely but my brain is always looking for whomever is missing.

Tell me I'm not the only one who does that?

NEEDING SUNLIGHT

There are reasons I don't live in Seattle or Dublin or the Midwest, or any place where it rains a lot. Well, it's not really about it raining a lot, because that doesn't bother me that much – it's about the cloud cover.

I need to see the sun. Even if it is bitterly cold outside, I need to see the sun. I guess it is all that vitamin D, I don't know. As a redhead, my parents were constantly smearing me from head to toe with sunscreen growing up, so I almost had to hate the sun because I always had to be protected from it.

But as I grew older and became in charge of my own sun protection I became less and less concerned about sunburn. Yes, it's an issue if I go someplace with a lot of reflection, like the beach, skiing, or anywhere there is sand. Yes, I still prefer to wear a hat while hiking or if I am going to be out in an open field. But by and large for short visits in the sun I don't put any sunscreen on. I just go and soak up the light.

Preferably with my bare feet on the ground at the same time and my kids thinking I am paying attention to them as they perform cartwheel after cartwheel after round-off.

My hubby and I really enjoy taking our cups of coffee or tea outside to drink on the deck or wander the yard and look at the plants in the morning to slowly wake up (this tends to be a weekend and day off activity). I enjoy taking walks in the morning while the sun is just creeping up.

I have even made my own sunscreen and need to make some more once we are done moving and I have a few minutes to do that kind of stuff. It makes a bit of a mess in the food processor so I have to schedule clean up time as well.

I don't put lots of sunscreen on my daughters, either. Some of them have their father's and my brother's skin tone and don't actually need it, they tan up so dark by the end of the summer in places it is hard to tell if they are clean or not.

My younger two are a bit more sensitive, but I still only put sunscreen on them when we are going to a location with reflection. It seems to work for us.

I have read all the data arguing both sides – that the sun is bad for you and that no, really, we need some unfiltered sunlight everyday to stay healthy.

I have been the parent who has not made sure that each and every one of my girls has been wearing a rasher and a hat to the beach. But then again, we aren't the stay-at-the-beach-all-day kind of family either. We are the stay-at-the-beach-for-a-couple-of-hours-by-which-point-everyone-is-tired-and-cranky-so-let's-go-back-home family.

That's okay. Last summer, before I broke my ankle, I took the girls to the lake every afternoon for about an hour to an hour and a half. I think they got more out of the regular visits to the water than they got from spending all day at a body of water but only doing it once a week or so.

But I have felt the judgment from other mothers for not having my kids "dressed appropriately" for the sun. I have seen it in the way they look at me while slathering on more sunscreen and tying the hat tighter on their child's head.

But it just doesn't work for my family. How else are you supposed to get enough vitamin D? There is no real proof that the D you drink in fortified milk or milk alternative products is really being absorbed well by your body. If that's the case, why do we all still get SAD in the winter?

Plus making vitamin D through your bare skin is free! Your body just knows how to do it, and does it while you are doing something else, like reading a book, gardening, or relaxing with a drink.

Maybe your kid does sunburn easily, so in that case do slather on the healthy sunscreen (not the cheap nasty stuff – remember, the skin is their largest organ!). But don't judge those of us who choose not to, who have children that maybe do not burn easily, who refuse to wear a hat at the beach so therefore we don't stay there all day, who let our children slowly build up their tans rather than having fights over the sunscreen.

We are all in this together, so why spend time judging? Feel free to pass the snacks you brought and if I need some sunscreen I will ask to borrow some.

In the meantime I am going to sit here in the sun, soak up the rays, and feel better.

HOMESCHOOLING CONFESSION: MY 12-YEAR-OLD CAN'T READ

Why is it that, as homeschoolers, we are held to a higher standard than others?

You know the whispers. "Is your kid socialized?" "How will they get a job and learn to get along with others?"

One I heard recently really hit home. They were talking about a child with learning disabilities and special needs who was being homeschooled and the comment was, "Why do those parents think they are expert enough to homeschool this child?" The implication being that they should send this special needs child to the experts at the school system. Don't get me started about how well that will work with the understaffing at schools, especially in the special needs department. Not to mention the labeling.

I grew up with a special needs brother. I suspect these days he would at the very least be put on the autism spectrum. He was a preemie, born early, so everything he does do is amazing. It was my normal. We were homeschooled partially because the so-called experts at school couldn't cope with his needs, and weren't really expert enough.

I get the judgment that goes on with the people outside the homeschooling world. I want to talk about the judgment that goes on inside the homeschooling world.

I remember being homeschooled back in the late '80s and '90s. If you weren't being homeschooled for religious reasons, you were just crazy. No one knew someone who was homeschooled back in those days, so we did certain things to not have to constantly answer questions. Like not going out during school hours to shops and things, other than the library, where they welcomed homeschoolers. I had a pen pal who wasn't even allowed to go in her own backyard during school hours so the neighbors wouldn't report them as truant – partially because they lived in a state where it was harder to homeschool.

And yes, I still look at states and their homeschooling laws before considering whether we would move there or not, if we needed to move. Certain states are just out, like Ohio and Pennsylvania, with their laws that are too restrictive.

Then there is the curriculum versus unschooling or cobbled-together-curriculum camps. I grew up unschooled, which is very much child-led, and in my mind, you learn what you need to learn when you need to learn it, both as a child and a grown-up. As long as you get there in the end, who cares if you learned to tie your shoes at 4 or 7?

But that seems to go out the window with reading. It is like the most important thing in early elementary and what the rest of the schooling is based on. Yet neurology points out that most kids' brains are not ready to learn to read (something we are not naturally hardwired to do, unlike, say, math and talking) until around age 8. But whether your kid is in school or not, if they are not reading by 8 you are failing as a parent.

I have four daughters. I struggled to learn to read and didn't do it for the joy of it until I was 11 or 12. You can't tell now, when I manage to read over 100 books a year for myself, not counting the picture books I read aloud. I got accepted to every college I applied to. I just needed way more phonics than they taught at the schools I went to early on.

My 12-year-old will tell you point-blank that she can't read - which isn't entirely true. She can read. It just isn't easy for her and she doesn't like it and she has a block in her brain about doing it. But she does read things in her world. She also hates phonics, and yes, she has been exposed to a lot of it. Her eyes and ears have been tested, and the only reason she would be classified at this point as dyslexic is that any child who makes it to 12 without reading well is labeled dyslexic. By the way, even the school system has illiterate kids, just a little behind her in age – as much as 40% at 3rd grade.

My 10-year-old reads better than the 12-year-old, though she is still behind her "grade level." But she has a passion for it and wants to work on reading regularly with me and reads picture books out loud to her younger sisters all the time.

My 7-year-old is finding reading wicked easy (I am not sure how she is doing it, I watch in wonder sometimes) and phonics makes so much sense for her. She hates to memorize the words that fall outside of it.

My 5-year-old is still working on writing her letters and isn't super interested in reading yet. She much prefers being read to at this point.

I get a lot of judgment about my 12-year-old though, especially from my homeschooling friends. I think they may be planning an intervention. Especially the one who also had a late reader and ended up sending him to school for extra reading help for a year and now he's doing better (as if it is an illness we all need to be cured from). But I know that if I send my daughter to any part of school at this point in the midst of preteen hormones and angst that she would curl up into a little ball and it would break her. If I wanted that I would have sent her to school to begin with.

It is getting so bad that I don't want to talk about it anymore. I have asked her Dad to work on it with her in case there is a personality issue. We have tried everything (infinite possibilities notwithstanding) and her brain just isn't there yet. I even recently got the dyslexia color reading things and she thought they were stupid and unhelpful so apparently she doesn't need them (however my 10- and 7-year-olds find they make reading faster when they use them).

I get tired of the questions about her. I get tired of feeling like I have to hide the fact that she isn't comfortable with reading, because that is really what it is – she can read, she just isn't comfortable doing it. She would much rather listen to audiobooks than read them. We even tried taking those away for a while and that just made everyone's life suck. And she is reading some adult audiobooks and upper YA books so she is getting all that exposure. Also her vocabulary is huge, so that isn't suffering.

I feel jealous of the parents whose kids just learned to read overnight, much like potty training. Only one of my kids did it herself and then in one weekend, which is how I supposedly did it. For everyone else, the process took much, much longer.

Yet I feel like even as I write this, you, the unknown reader, are going to be judging me on this failing of education. I could defensively point out that she is well-socialized, active in Girl Scouts, has even earned her public speaking badge, and is an amazing duck whisperer and maker of things. That she understands relationships between people and gets math super easily.

But that doesn't change the feeling. That doesn't change the feeling of needing to hide. That I am getting judged on not teaching my daughter to read, or not providing enough resources, or just plain not sending her to school so they can beat it into her. I am sure someone would say if I had fewer children I could give her more time. Though she probably gets the most time of all my daughters at the moment.

Why do we judge each other so? Every kid has something they are not great at. Every human has gaps in their knowledge and education no matter what system they are in. I have always felt that by keeping her in a loving environment so that she could grow naturally I am helping her be a more resilient adult.

But the older she gets, the more crushing the weight feels. I don't want to have us both in tears every day over this. I know she is fully capable of learning to read when she is ready. And sometimes the highly intelligent do things their own way, too.

SEASONS OF OUR LIVES

HOT - I'M MELTING

It is so hot here in rural Maine. It's early this year. It isn't even the 4th of July yet and it is so hot. Which means that we are all cranky, irritable, and it is even harder to use our nice voices to each other.

Yet we must use our nice voices, at least part of the time. We need to speak with kindness and understand that the others are just as tired as we are.

I announced last night that I at least am running siesta hours starting today. Well, I probably won't start until tomorrow because I have a friend coming to help me unpack part of the house today around 11 am, so it depends on how long she stays.

Anyway, my kids are in a bit of a revolt. I explained that the idea was that you get up early in the morning (not that I am waking them up early, mind you, but I am getting up early) and you get things done for a while, and then around the hottest part of the day, you lay down and read or sleep or just color and hang out until the hottest part of the day passes, and then you get up and do more things, and you stay up later at night than you usually do. We have had no luck getting the kids to even think about going to sleep before full dark this past week anyway. That siesta time in the middle of the day is how you keep from burning out and how you get rid of some of the cranky irritable feelings.

We will see. Like I said, I am not sure it is going to work today, but you better believe I am making this happen on the 4th. Especially since we are planning on getting up super early to go pick strawberries. We will all need that lie-down afterward.

So far the biggest complaint I have heard is that they couldn't possibly go to sleep during the hottest part of the day because they can't go to sleep at night as it is. Which isn't totally true. As soon as they convince themselves to just wear big oversized t-shirts, to put a wet washcloth (or flannel as my mother-in-law calls it) on their head and stop fussing, they fall straight to sleep.

I figure the absolute worst case is that I will let them watch TV while I have my lie-down in the middle of the day. But I really like the idea of them lying down and listening to audiobooks, or coloring, or reading books, or otherwise having time alone and separate from everyone else.

I think that may be the only way we survive this first summer further inland where I don't know where any of the local swimming holes are yet (though they are allowed to spend as much time in the sprinkler as they want now that we are on a well) and where I still feel like unpacking and organizing is a higher priority than most anything else, outside of getting my work done.

They are of course completely over the whole idea of having to do any more unpacking, moving, or hauling stuff up and down stairs as we find things. We still have more things out in our yard and driveway than I would like, and I am hoping to convince them to haul some of it down into the basement today, because after all it is pretty cool down there.

I think I will hold the popsicles and ice cream cones ransom for some help. That seems fair, right? You get all hot and sweaty doing some heavy lifting and then you get a nice cold thing to put in your mouth and cool down with.

Thank goodness we have a dishwasher because it is way too hot for anyone to want to do the dishes, though I do have some pans I am going to need to do soon. Also I think I should make some pasta salad today and keep it in the fridge. That way when people get hungry or don't like enough of dinner, or whatever, they can have something cold to eat.

I suggested the pasta salad plan at dinner last night and the kids thought I was crazy. I think maybe I haven't done this before, so they don't know what they are missing. Maybe I should do some potato salad too. I have an instant pot, so I don't even need to make the whole kitchen hot while boiling potatoes.

Of course, we are also seriously looking into getting a grill. Our new house actually has a special carved-out spot on the deck just off the kitchen to hold a grill. We have a charcoal one, but a gas one seems so much simpler and faster for average dinner cooking. My hubby is actually looking at one of those combination ones that does propane, charcoal, and has a smoker attachment. I just like the idea of cooking outside. Grilled veggies sounds so good.

Well, my first kiddo has gotten up, so I should get the rest of my work done. Hopefully this siesta thing will work. Having lived in Europe in the summer where no one has AC, I really think it's the only way to get through the summer. It also helps to remember what it feels like when you are just trying to get through the winter later, right?

The kids whine either way. I keep trying to tell them you can't control the weather, so don't let the weather control your mood.

IT'S SO STICKY

It's so sticky. It is *wake up in the morning already drenched in sweat that won't evaporate* kind of sticky. A little bit of miserable to start your day.

Yesterday it was supposed to rain, and it did, finally. Of course it started as we were leaving a library program and needed to walk across town to the only parking space we had been able to find for the van. It looked like we were going to get drenched, but in the end it was just enough rain to get you wet and for the kids to start complaining about how cold it was, but not enough to actually drench anyone. Just enough to be annoying. It was worse at times on the drive home.

I thought the rain was going to cause the humidity to leave the air and for the temperatures to go down. Apparently the weather was messing with me, because this morning, it's only about 18 hours after the last rain and it feels like it is going to be another bruiser of a hot day. The humidity is already there. While I am considering a shower, I am not sure what the point would be, as I'm sure my current layer of sweat is just going to coat all of me again a few minutes after I step out of the shower.

The kids are starting to ramp up wanting to go to the beach. I totally get their request. I am just 1) not sure they all know where their swimsuits are and 2) am hosting an open house later this week and still have a few more rooms to organize and straighten up. My hope is to have all the rooms done by Friday evening and then Saturday morning can just be things like sweeping, a quick mop around, and wiping down the bathrooms. I'll get the kids to run the vacuum upstairs, where I am not showing off my house, but it needs it anyway.

Because I had a virtual summit last week for my work, the kids are already a bit annoyed at me being so busy cleaning and unpacking in the late afternoon. Because the one library that we go to for some reason decided to schedule all of their programing this week, we have activities there three days this week, which is also just something that happens.

Then there is the problem of my not knowing where any of the swimming holes actually are up here. I know where Damariscotta Lake is, but it's not my favorite because it's a state park and usually pretty crowded. Beyond that, I don't have any idea.

While my hubby and the kids have all met the neighbors, I haven't yet, though I suspect she is probably the perfect person to ask where the swimming holes are. But doing that means that I then have the information and can't put off going any longer, right?

I am thinking next week we can start checking out the swimming holes. I had a good routine last summer where the swimming hole was about ten minutes away and we would go every late afternoon for about an hour and then come back home. Ducks swam in this lake, so the girls were pretty happy, and it was a good spot where I could sit and read and keep an eye on them.

I am willing to do that again this year, just not this week. We still have the house to get ready, and I am already out every day with activities for them and then picking up their grandmother on Friday. So perhaps next week will work better. My mother can come or stay depending on how she is feeling, and I can work to have dinner planned ahead of time.

That could most definitely work. In the meantime we have a sprinkler. Our well has super cold water coming out of it so we think it must be dug pretty deep, and the water flow is good. The ducks need their water changed and refilled several times a day, so there are already those built-in opportunities to get wet. Maybe those things will work.

I don't think I can convince hubby to go to the water this weekend. After our party Saturday night we are just going to want to clean up on Sunday. We might be having a new baby come and visit us, or we might not. It may just need to be a *lounge around the house* kind of day.

That could totally work.

For me, anyway.

I'm not sure how my hot and sticky children will feel. Especially since we are now out of ice cream and we haven't found enough pieces to put the popsicle maker together yet. Maybe I can find that tomorrow as I finish unpacking and organizing the kitchen?

It's a thought, anyway, as we unpack, one box at a time.

HALLOWEEN COSTUMES MIGHT JUST KILL ME

It is that time of year again. Immediately upon taking down all the *Back to School* shit (and sometimes even before that) they put up all the Halloween costumes. I think it was supposed to coincide with pumpkin lattes being released originally, but now it just seems to be whenever the company that owns the store decides to rotate stock.

Then it becomes even more impossible to shop with your kids. It's a bit like a prequel to Christmas, when your kids always want to go down the Christmas aisles to see all the ornaments and you feel like the mothers in *A Miracle on 34th Street*, who really do not want to stand in line to see Santa Claus or buy any more presents.

Halloween is like the prequel to that, to get you ready for all the commercialism of Christmas. It seems to start with the candy – and early. I was in Sam's Club in August and they had big jugs of Halloween pretzels to pass out to trick-or-treaters. The pretzels were shaped like jack-o-lanterns and bats. I had to buy them, of course, on the off chance that we actually get some trick-or-treaters in the new house, and on the even better chance that my kids will eat them as snacks when we need to take car trips.

But beyond the candy, and how that either all gets eaten in one night or sticks around for the rest of the year, and seeing sugar everywhere, there are the costumes.

Oh my gawd - the costumes. Thank goodness my kids don't go to school and really do not have a lot of opportunity to compare notes with other kids. Because here's the thing: I am one crafty mama. I could totally Pinterest up the stuff I make, but frankly my house is never that clean and the lighting is usually dark because it is after the kids go to bed. So it just doesn't happen.

But here is the problem with being a crafty mama. I have four kids. That could mean four unique handmade costumes every fucking year, that they are only going to wear for a couple of hours at most, right? Because yes, my girls do love to play dress up, but no, they would much rather put on bigger people's clothes than wear actually costumes that anyone took the time to make. Seriously.

So I have the skills. But I do not have the interest or the time. And since my kiddos got some theater-grade costume hand-me-downs years ago, I decided I am not doing costumes. *You have plenty of costumes already taking up floor space around the house, you are creative, you can figure this out.* I am willing to be a sounding board and help you think about how you can do things, but I am not, no way, going to help you. You've got that yourself.

This has worked for years. My eldest is 12, after all. Beyond occasionally dressing up myself (and only if I absolutely have to) I have been uninvolved in costuming, and it's been great.

But then my youngest announced about six months before Halloween that she wanted to dress up as Draco Malfoy from Harry Potter. She is perfect for it, with long blond hair that can be swept back, and she has the personality of a Slytherin to a tee. But we do not have any cloaks and Harry Potter–type costume stuff, because my kids have never shown an interest before.

I talked to her about making a Slytherin scarf to go with her costume. I even found a free pattern on the web and my mother offered to start it while she was visiting this summer. She probably got about 18 inches of the scarf done. But here's the thing. I hate knitting scarves, and I have other handwork projects going right now.

This same child had her first birthday party this year, when she turned five, and the guest list was small enough that I made all the kids either unicorn headbands or bear headbands depending on the gender. So there is no way in hell that scarf is getting done by Halloween – or actually before, because it's on a Wednesday this year so Halloween takes place the Saturday before in most cases. Especially when I discovered that Target had a better one complete with fringe and the actual Slytherin coat of arms for $7. So I ordered that instead, to go with the Slytherin shirt we bought her months ago for her birthday.

Of course, being five, after months of saying she was going to be Draco Malfoy for Halloween, the closer we get to it the less she seems to be willing to dress up as Draco. It is enough to drive a parent insane.

Meanwhile, my 10-year-old didn't get a cool headband for the birthday party, because I was doing the birthday girl and guests first. So she needs me to finish up gray cat ears for her before I leave in 36 hours to be gone for 72 hours, because she might be going to a Halloween party while I am gone. I have already made fox ears for the 6-year-old. Thank goodness the 12-year-old seems unimpressed. I am unimpressed. How did I manage to get roped into helping with costumes this year?

How can I make it stop?

Because they just might kill me. Halloween costumes. They just might do me in. I've been hearing about all my crafty and non-crafty friends making them for their kids. I don't want to spend my money on buying them the cheap nasty costumes in the store (because you know how I feel about shopping with my kids, period). I think I should just hide and declare Halloween over. *Here's a bunch of candy, go get the child's version of a hangover, and I'll see you tomorrow morning.*

Yep, that sounds like a great idea!

THANKSGIVING CRISIS

We had a lovely Thanksgiving this year. We spent it at a friend's home. There were 20 people at the table, including some international exchange students who were experiencing their first American Thanksgiving.

We had stayed late to play games, the kids watched Christmas movies, and we had a really cozy time, though all the adults were pretty tired by then. I reminded all of my girls to go to the bathroom before we left their house, as it is at least a 45-minute drive and with the dark and snowy road conditions (from a storm earlier in the week) it was probably going to take longer.

My youngest had been pretty enamored of the bubbly water my friend could make from her sodastream, and had been drinking quite a lot of it. I hadn't paid too much attention, because I did not realize how late it had gotten (when it gets dark at 4 pm anyway, it's hard to tell if it's 6 or 8), or I would have maybe had a premonition of what was going to happen.

Less than 10 minutes from my friend's house my youngest declared that she needed to pee. This wasn't just something she was saying to be annoying, she well and truly had the whole *unable to sit still* thing going on in the back seat.

But this is Thanksgiving night in rural Maine. We don't go by a lot of gas stations on a good day as it is, and this is at almost 9 pm. Where can I possibly take her to pee? We asked if she would pee out the door, and even pulled over. I was prepared to hold her and let her pee off my lap out the door rather than having her squat outside. But being the sensible child she is, she was having none of that.

It finally dawned on me that one of the few places that is always open is the hospital, which we were going right by. Not something I would have normally come up with, but they are always open, right? My hubby nicely drove us and parked the car but refused to come in with us. I made all the girls get out, because this isn't my first rodeo, and if one girl needs to pee, they should all try.

The ER was the only door open since it was after 8 pm, but this is a small rural hospital and it was deserted and quiet. We went in and I called out that we didn't have an emergency, we just really needed the bathroom.

The woman behind the desk couldn't have been any nicer. She smiled and buzzed us into the hospital and told my girls that they always have a bathroom available to be used. So off we stomped to the nearest family bathroom where we all went in and I answered questions as to why there was a shower in the bathroom and why there was a *pull if you need help* cord by the toilet.

We said thank you on our way out, and were getting back into the van just as the ambulance was pulling in with just its lights on.

I was mentally patting myself on the back for a crisis averted. But I was too soon.

Less than 20 minutes later, after we had decided to take the long way home in hopes of only traveling well-plowed roads, my youngest was once again doing the wiggle. She had to pee. Only this time there really was no place to stop (and all the gas stations we had passed were closed anyway). She was so miserable and there was nothing to be done, even though I did offer that she could pee outside the car again.

She ended up pissing herself. Her relief was obvious, and within two minutes she was asleep. I had to deal with changing her and washing her car seat after we got home. But that relief was such a release for all of us, as her upset was so hard to be a witness to without the ability to do anything about it.

This was not how I wanted to end Thanksgiving. But once again, I think it is important to tell these stories. Because I suspect we have all had similar circumstances. She felt so much better when she stopped fighting what her body needed her to do, and really it wasn't that big of a deal to clean up. When was the last time you let your body do what it needed to?

INTENTIONAL HOLIDAYS

It's that time of year again. When our kids go slightly crazy in anticipation of the big day, of getting presents galore, of time off from school, and of spending more time with you. Doing all the holiday things, whatever that means to your family, whether it be parties, decorating trees, caroling, watching football games, or whatever the holiday season means to you and yours.

But it also feels like a super-easy recipe for disaster, with sugar at every corner and therefore the temptation to overindulge, both for us and our cute little kids that then suddenly turn into brats. It is a bit like the holiday parade I was part of this year as a Girl

Scout leader. Almost all of my troop was there, a total of seven girls, only two of which were mine. We were all riding on a float that they had helped decorate with 37 other girls from other troops in the area. What made it a leader's nightmare was the pick up time, as with this particular parade it just stops on Main Street and the parents come to the float and want to take their kids. As you can imagine, 44 girls getting picked up at once on a multi-sided float can make leaders who need to see parents' eyeballs super antsy.

It worked out well this year, as there was as single exit from the float and I had prepped all the parents and the kids that I had to see their eyeballs before they could walk away with their girls. As near as I could tell, all the other leaders had similar experiences with their parents, because we prepared them and the girls ahead of time for what we expected to have happen at the float.

But what about the craziness of the holidays? Can you prepare your family in advance to have a smoother time? Can you prepare self-care for yourself around it so that you can be vigilant when you need to be (like when there are 44 girls on a float that need to stay seated while you cruise down Main Street) but also get some time to relax and enjoy the holidays too?

How can you do this? Here are some things that I have done in the past and am trying out this year to help navigate through this season of light.

Every year my kids and I sit down and come up with a list of activities we want to do, usually from Thanksgiving through Christmas. What is great about this is that I get a chance to find out what each of my kids want to do and what is important to them. So if, say, nobody wants to go see *The Nutcracker* again, we don't have to go. We instead have time to try some other things, like attending a historical 19th-century Christmas celebration and going to see the *Christmas in Arendalle* that a library we have never been to is hosting. I like to put the list on post-it notes, so we can move them around on the calendar as needed, as sledding in the snow is weather contingent and we have already watched a Christmas movie as a family this year.

So step one is being really conscious of what we say yes to, schedule-wise. Right now I have all the Saturdays between now and Christmas scheduled with an activity, and we know the approximate date we are going to go and get our Christmas tree. Any additional invites will be filtered through the already-busy Saturdays. It can be easier to say "no, we already have plans" sometimes than just saying "no."

I do try and keep us busy just before Christmas, because that countdown to Christmas morning can be a frenzy, and that's just my younger two. The weekend before Christmas is the one weekend where we currently have an event on Saturday and a party on Sunday. With Christmas being on a Tuesday this year, I am hoping my hubby can work from home on Christmas Eve and if the weather is good I can keep the kids outside most of the time.

I also have the ability to take the week before Christmas off, so I am not working after December 14th until the 2nd of January, because it's just too crazy with little ones, and frankly, in five years they will be old enough that I can work then if I want to. I want to enjoy the delight of Christmas while I still can, before they are too old to care.

I also try and take care of Christmas cards and the like early. We make a holiday calendar for the extended family, and I usually build that on Thanksgiving weekend so that it is ready to be ordered when the sale is on, and then they get mailed out as soon as I have them. I often also write the Christmas letters and cards and order the photos around Thanksgiving, too.

This year for Thanksgiving we were super tired, so I didn't worry about working on that and instead just really focused on rest and relaxation with my family. But I will get the cards out early so that they are done. I totally think my friend who did New Year's cards last year was smart. She didn't even try and get them out for Christmas, and that took a lot of pressure off.

I have also been working on Christmas gift shopping since probably July. My kids know that they have to let me know what they want from Santa by Halloween so the elves have time to make it. None of this last-minute request stuff. Because I use Swagbucks to pay for a lot of Christmas gifts, not quite everything is in the house yet, but most of it is, and I know how much is left to order at the beginning of December.

That just leaves some food shopping and maybe a few things for stockings. But I have already been talking to the family about what we want for Christmas dinner and have gotten a few of the things for the relish tray for lunch already squirreled away in the cupboard. By working ahead I can spread the cost out as well as feel less stressed and I can just focus on doing what the kids want to do as we wait for the day.

How do you prepare for the season? Have you thought about what you are going to say to any rude relatives or acquaintances? Have you thought about how much space you really have in your schedule for holding social events? Have you gotten the teacher/scout leaders/postal worker gifts sorted, or at least have ideas? I like to get my kids involved in the making of those things so we can work on them together and they are also part of the gift-giving process.

ELVING

Every year I try to move away from gifts of things and toward experiences as gifts.

This is hard to do with kids. They want things they can hold and touch and taste and smell. I want a less-cluttered house. Or stuff they will use, and things that won't break right away.

It can be a hard balance. A few years ago I tried giving digital classes and the supplies needed for those classes. That really didn't go over well.

We have had holidays themed by puzzles, games, graphic novels and adult coloring books, and even Legos. This year, however, there was no theme, as there was nothing that all of the kids wanted. Just a few specific things they each wanted.

Some of my kids are getting art supplies. All of them are getting a craft kit with a new craft they have never tried. A few are getting books (but not all of them). They are all getting socks and PJs and leggings or tights.

All of them are getting a fun novelty hat I have made them. There is a fox cowl coming, two kinds of unicorn hats, a duck hat that I still have to make, and maybe even a BB8. We will just have to wait and see what we can find.

They made whipped body butter for their Girl Scout leaders because it was something they could all help make. I am making a series of the same sewed items for my relatives and friends, and I am not quite half way done (three of them are staying in the house, so that works). There is a sweater for one daughter and an apron for another coming from my Mom.

One of my daughters is making homemade playdough for all of her sisters. Another daughter made some for her Secret Santa in her Girl Scout troop. I believe there may be some drawn pictures coming my way for the holidays.

At least not everything has been bought. A lot has been made. Many of the traditions of the holidays for us are around food that we make together. Wish Bread on the longest night, St. Lucia buns for breakfast tomorrow for the old date of the Solstice, pork pies and coffee cake for Christmas Day, fondue for New Year's Eve, and probably some carnitas for the week in between. We make as much as possible as a family, together, and that, more than the decorations, is what makes the holidays for us. My hubby and I almost always brew a batch of beer on Christmas Day after the gifts have been opened and the kids are busy. There is usually a long game to be played on the longest night.

What traditions make the holidays for you?

⊗

311

'TWAS THE WEEK BEFORE CHRISTMAS

'Twas the week before Christmas and all through the house...

My children were going crazy! How about yours? I planned to take this week off so I can be with them as much as possible, because they are just a little crazy this time of year. Especially my younger two. There is just something about the amp-up for Christmas, and Solstice is this week as well.

I have activities planned. We got together with friends yesterday and melted peppermint candies into candy bowls and made ornaments. Our last Girl Scout meeting until after the New Year is tonight. We are going to see *The Nutcracker* on Friday. They are getting a long game to play on Thursday for the Solstice. We have holiday music, baking, and games to play.

My personal ideal for the last week before the holidays would be: reading books, listening to audiobooks while finishing up the last few handmade gifts (for friends and a few left for family), watching a few movies, going for walks or hikes as the weather allows, maybe decorating. Making some warm cozy drinks.

My kids' ideas? Hot chocolate, more playing in snow if we get some more, counting down the seconds until Santa comes, *can we have another play date?* Making stuff. *Have I gotten something for my sister yet? Can we make and eat more cookies?*

Thank goodness there is only a week left! We will survive this. I promise.

SNOW DAYS

Snow days used to be fun. They used to be highly anticipated days off from school, where the idea in your head was that you either got to sit in front of the TV watching your favorite movies and shows or got out and build massive snowmen, forts, and tunnels with your siblings and friends and then come inside for hot cocoa and maybe the cookies your mom was making while you were out in the snow.

But these days, as a parent, snow days don't seem that much fun. If you are working, then you have an unexpected day of the kids being home from school that you have to manage somehow, as well as possibly making it to work yourself.

If you work from home, you don't have to take the day off, and if you have clients in other geographical areas, it doesn't often make sense to take the day off. But the internet is going to slow down, because everybody else's kids are going to be on Netflix or Facebook or otherwise taking up the load.

Oh and let's not forget that your kiddos are going to want to go outside in all that snow, as soon as they can see it. So that means finding all their snow gear, and then getting them ready and dealing with the bathroom and then finally shoving them outside. To have them come back inside in less than 10 minutes, complaining of broken sleds, cold noses, and surely that hot cocoa is made?

Of course it's not because you spent that not-quite-ten-minutes recovering from shoving them all in clothes. Maybe you had the energy to pour yourself another cup of coffee or pop a piece of chocolate from your hidden stash in your mouth. But to actually make cocoa and cookies? Nope, you didn't even begin to get to that. And do you really want to?

I mean, feeding your kids sugar after they have just come back inside is a recipe for them to start bouncing off the walls of the already too-small-feeling house, and really, do you want to encourage that kind of behavior? It almost always leads to tears - yours or theirs, but someone is going to cry. Yep, sugar crashes always leads to crying.

What about warm soup to feed them for lunch? Well, only half of my kids even like soup so I am not convinced that is a good idea, because who really wants to see your kids wear soup anyway?

By the time all the squabbling and complaining over the lack of hot cocoa and cookies has subsided, by the time they are out of all that gear and have warmed up those cute little red noses of theirs, they are ready to go back outside again. Unless you are unlucky (or maybe lucky) and this is a blizzard with really cold temperatures and your kids actually don't want to go back outside. That is always possible.

Ah, snow days. I dream of hygge-inspired days of being curled up in bed or a comfy chair with a nice warm drink, some healthy but tasty snacks, some good music or a movie and a good book as well as a satisfying knitting, crocheting, or hand-sewing project. I don't consider sewing badges on vests to be one of those projects.

Maybe having a lazy conversation with my hubby. Maybe playing a tabletop game or two (but I mean, if I actually did that with my kids, it would end in tears, because see above sugar crash, not to mention they are not good sportswomen yet, at all). Maybe the cat curled up on my lap. Yep, that's my dream.

My fantasy.

Not, of course, the reality of snow days.

Nope. Those include wet socks, mittens, and hats strewn all over my house, as well as ever-increasing small piles of snow in my house slowly melting.

Which is why I actually like shoveling snow now.

My kids prefer to stay inside lest I insist that they help.

So I get all that time it takes me to shovel alone. By myself. With maybe an audiobook to listen to, or maybe just silence.

That's the best part about snow days.

Shoveling in silence.

WEATHER WITH YOU

I truly believe you can't control the weather.

So why get upset by it? I mean, it's just weather, and you are either prepared for it, or you're not and you have to scramble and get prepared for it.

And yes, I have lived through hurricanes. So I know that weather can be contrary and devastating and downright annoying.

Most of the time I don't waste any energy being annoyed or angry at it. I don't have that many fucks to give as it is – why waste it on the weather?

But this extended winter this year in Maine is beginning to really get under my skin and sit on the last of my nerves.

I knew the prediction going into the winter was that we were going to be front-loaded, and we were going to get a lot of snow and colder weather earlier in the season than we sometimes do. Here in midcoast Maine, sometimes we don't get any real snow until after the January thaw, when everyone acts like we are not going to get any winter at all and then we get slammed in February. But not this year.

This year we had cabin fever by January because not only were we buried in snow but we also had such wicked cold weather that it was too cold for the kids to go outside and sled in said snow or do anything other than their chores of looking after the ducks. It hurt your face to be outside, and it's hard to convince the babies you love to go outside when their faces hurt. Just sayin.'

But I had made the erroneous assumption that being front-loaded for the winter meant that maybe it would get better by March, that maybe we would have one of those early Marches where everyone goes to the beach before the end of the month.

Nope. We continued to get snow in March. We have continued to get snow in April. We have gotten sleet and hail after the fifteenth of April this year. And I am getting tired of it.

We unfortunately (though at the time it seemed like a wonderful act of God) had some lovely weather a week or so ago and the kids were outside, wanting to get their bikes out (but the ground wasn't ready for those tire treads) and building and just hanging out in the duck pen for hours.

It was awesome. It was like a reminder that life could get quiet again because all four of my daughters could be outside playing. Not needing me, and making all the noise their little hearts need to make, and I was actually able to think a straight thought on my own.

So getting slammed by more wet yucky weather is like when a toddler deprives you of sleep for more than two nights in a row. I am just irrationally angry at the whole Goddamn world. Like, seriously, what the fuck is wrong with the world?

I don't have a basement, and my house is currently an unspeakable mess because I have had four kids locked up in it for five months now! With the few warm spells we have had, they have tracked buckets of mud in my house as well, and even though we have swept, and swept, and washed (so much for a stay-cation last week with hubby) it still feels like there is a layer of mud and grime on everything.

Now, I understand the importance of mud season. I love eating my fruits and veggies as much as the next person, maybe even more so as there are only a few I won't eat (I'm looking at you, okra), but oh my God, as a mother I hate mud season. I just hate it. For the love of all that is holy I would be happy to never have to deal with another mud season ever again.

By and large my girls are past the need to make mud pies. But they still track in mud on their shoes and bodies. I need an airlock chamber with a hose and a shower. That would be my perfect world, so that the mud never made it past that airlock chamber. Because in most houses here in Maine, the door you use opens right into the kitchen.

Which means that's where the mud ends up – and no one wants to eat mud with their food.

So even though most of the time the weather really doesn't bother me, this spring (which is beyond drunk and belligerent) needs to go either back to bed and wake up when it is ready to be serious or can just get its act together and stay warm. I can only imagine what this is doing for the maple syrup production this year.

Seriously, may the mud stay in the duck pen (because like pigs, they love it) and may it forever stay out of my house.

Because this *wait 5 minutes the weather will change* shit is just not working this year.

HIKING WITH KIDS

My family loves to hike. I know that might sound crazy if your family doesn't even like to go for a walk, but my family does.

It helps that my hubby and I both like to hike in the woods and grew up doing it either with our family or as part of scouts or school. When we were first married, we lived in southern Florida where it was very hot and we would go to the mall or Ikea to get a walk in, in the air conditioning, because otherwise we couldn't drink enough water to stay hydrated to walk outside.

But once we moved to Maine, with at that time our 4- and 2-year-olds, we started taking them out on hikes. In the beginning it was hard to go very far because I was the only one who could carry a child (thanks to a back injury for my husband), and at two and four neither of my daughters had very strong legs.

But we kept it up, often just taking walks on the road rather than going in the woods so that someone could be in the stroller and someone could be on my back if needed. Then we moved to town and at that point we only had one car so we walked to the library or town all the time. As our family grew, who was walking and who was riding or being carried changed, of course.

Over time we moved again and got closer to one of the state parks as well as made more frequent camping trips up to Acadia National Park. Our girls got better at hiking. We also discovered that our eldest, who was really beginning to hit the throes of hormones and being a preteen, was so much happier and better-behaved in the days that followed if we went on a hike. It has almost become a prescription for family happiness going on a hike every weekend when there isn't snow on the trails.

We have been hiking up the local mountain with a summit of over 800 feet, and a three-mile trail up and back, most weekends since 2015. My third child has grown up hiking that trail, and at ages 4 and 5 still got tired and needed help at some points. Her younger sister, on the other hand, has been hiking that trail by herself since she was three, only needing a ride down the last quarter of the mountain last year after hiking all the way up.

It helps that in July and August blueberries can be found as you get to the upper portions of the trail. My hubby loves to eat the wild blueberries, so the kids have learned that if at all possible they should try and beat him up to the blueberry spots.

Last year in early August, while bringing a friend along with us, I managed to slip on some wet rocks and break my ankle. That put our hiking on hold for a while.

This spring I have been walking in the morning (often to just get some quiet moments to myself as well as some exercise) and periodically we walk with the girls as a family as well.

This Sunday is Mother's Day and the weather is good so we are going to go back up the mountain again. Winter was late leaving this year, and with other things going on, like Scouts and home buying, this is our first real opportunity to go back up the hill.

I know it will take us a little bit longer than it will as we keep doing it. It will be interesting to see who ends up being in the back with me (it tends to rotate throughout our hiking season, with each kid having hikes where they are in the back for at least part of it) as I have more patience with starts and stops and whining than my husband.

We are planning to take the yearly mother-daughter photographs at the summit this year for a change. It is our one tradition for Mother's Day – you have to pose for photos with me. So as they get older it is something they have always done so they can just shut up and smile.

I am looking forward to the stress relief that comes from walking in the woods. The happiness my children find from being on a path and seeing how the path has changed this year from last. Having them carry more of the water this year and sharing a snack when we reach the summit.

It seems like a great way to officially celebrate that there are more warmer days than cooler ones finally and a way to see how everyone has grown.

Plus it will be nice to hike up that trail again without any major injuries!

MOTHER'S DAY

There can be so much angst over one special Sunday in the year. It doesn't help that there's this huge commercial pitch the likes of which I think only Valentine's Day can compete with. Get mom flowers, get her a card, and make her day special. Take her out to dinner because you can't cook, and spoil her with chocolate – every mom loves chocolate.

Then as I jokingly (but not really) told my husband as we were climbing up a hill on this Mother's Day, it is like one of the few days of the year where the competition gets fierce on social media. Whose kids made the cutest Mother's Day cards? Who had breakfast in bed? Whose hubby went over the top with showering them with gifts?

Whose teenagers tagged them in soppy posts? Who has a newborn and therefore didn't get any sleep whatsoever? Don't forget the moms who have lost their children. Don't forget your own mom even if she has passed on. Don't forget your mother-in-law, and the women in your life that act as surrogate moms...

On and on and on.

A good day to avoid social media, don't you think?

My mother-in-law never made a big deal over Mother's Day, because she expected her boys to love her and treat her with respect all the time, not just one day of the year.

I think my Mom had a similar opinion, though I did usually try and get her something or make her a card. Buying flowers to pot is pretty standard.

I have always told my hubby that Mother's Day is really supposed to be from the kids, so whatever is age appropriate for them is fine, like sloppy wet kisses and handmade drawings. All I want him to do is cook dinner that day, which is pretty normal because he cooks most weekend dinners anyway.

I do ask all my girls to pose for a photograph as a group and individually with me on Mother's Day. And believe me, some years that is more than enough, especially if they don't do the whole photos thing anymore (which seems to happen at multiple ages by the way). This year my youngest was having none of it and was standing where she thinks she is out of the photo. But those still make great shots to remember next year.

This year, since we are in the middle of home buying hell, I asked the kids to get me some wind chimes after we move. They have to sound pretty and look nice, with the emphasis on sounding pretty (so many wind chimes look nice but sound awful). On Sunday my 9-year-old brought me down a coloring page she had colored, folded up, and wrote *To Mummy I Love You* on. I asked her to put her name and age on the back because I do keep my Mother's Day artwork and it can be hard to tell who did what after a few years.

None of my other daughters made me anything special. Which is fine. Totally fine. I asked that we get up and go climb Mount Battie on Mother's Day, with a stop to get coffee on the way. I cooked everyone made-to-order-duck-eggs for breakfast and we got to the park between 9 and 10 am. At one point my youngest lost her shit, which is normal; someone always does. She found it soon enough again (having all the black flies biting her seemed to convince her that if she just kept walking they would go away again – which happened and for days since she has blamed every bug bite on stopping too long on our hike) and we continued on. I got photos at the top, and we had bread and water and peanut butter before heading back down.

Our timing was perfect. Just as we were getting off the trail everyone else who thought going on a hike with their mother was a great idea was arriving. We were back in the car by noon, which was great as we had the whole rest of the day at home.

I even got a short nap and time to read my book in bed for a little while that afternoon. It was a good day.

I remember the Mother's Days and birthdays where I have still had to clean wet sheets, mop up vomit, change diapers, and do dishes. I am grateful for any day I don't have to do that. It doesn't matter if it happens on the special day marked for mothers. Because let's face it, once you become a mother you are always a mother, no matter what happens to your child. You have given birth to your heart outside of your body (maybe even multiple times) and your life has changed in fundamental ways.

So I raise a glass to all the mothers out there: the new mothers, the mothers who have been riding this rodeo for a while, and the ones whose kids no longer reside in their homes. So much love to you. Know that you are not alone when you are cleaning up the mess and the shit, and keeping those people alive (I hear it gets worse the older they get).

We are here for you. You are surrounded by a Rebellion of women who are in this together. We've got your back. We are shining little beacons of hope. This too will pass. You will find sleep again. You are an amazing mother!

EPILOGUE

Are you ready to join the rebellion? I have created an online group in Discord (a social app) where you can connect with other like minded mothers in a judgement free environment, and the great thing about Discord is you only have to follow the threads (#) you are interested in.

To get access to this exclusive community first please fill out our quick questionnaire here and then we will send you the link to invite you to our community!

https://forms.gle/Ddmam3QfzB9ZSGzv8

ABOUT THE AUTHOR

Chase Young is an author, Girl Scout Leader, entrepreneur, maker and mother to four daughters currently 12, 10, 7 & 5. She wrote this book because she was tired of hearing how tired all the mothers in her community were feeling. Of having discussions about how you can ask for help and it can get better and just getting back blank stares. How we all feel so much better when we can laugh at the crazy shit our kids/spouses/pets just did. Chase wrote this book so mothers can feel supported no matter how their mothering journey is currently going. Chase needed permission to ask for help -- and had to get over the fear that everyone was going to judge her for being imperfect (but little did she know they all felt the same as she did).

By learning to ask and RECEIVE help Chase was able to start to breathe again, and become a much better mom because of that. You don't have to do it their way, your kids can go to bed early or stay up late and you can do it the way that works best for your family. You can take care of yourself and your family will be better for it, and that's what being a Rebel Mom is all about.

Made in the USA
San Bernardino, CA
18 June 2019